101 TIPS FOR A ZERO-WASTE KITCHEN

Also by Kathryn Kellog
101 Ways to Go Zero Waste

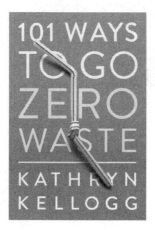

101 TIPS
FOR A
ZERO-WASTE
KITCHEN

KATHRYN KELLOGG

Countryman Press

An Imprint of W. W. Norton & Company
Independent Publishers Since 1923

This book is intended as a general information resource. The author is neither a dietician nor a food science expert. This book includes directions for creating vinegar by means of fermentation. Fermenting at home carries certain risks, including, but not limited to, contamination of foods from inadequate cleaning or sanitization of equipment and allergic reactions to ingredients. Please be sure to read and familiarize yourself with the fermentation directions and warnings in the book.

Please pay careful attention to the warnings about how long you can safely store different foods in different ways (e.g., in the fridge and/or in an airtight container) before they are no longer edible. Storage times suggested are average times based on ideal storage conditions. If you do not properly dehydrate ingredients in recipes that call for dehydrated ingredients, then those foods will go bad before the end of the recommended storage period. Also, please be sure to note the book's warnings about mold. As a general rule, if mold is visible on a food item, if a fruit or vegetable is disintegrating, or if a food item smells bad, do not eat it or use it.

The commercial products that the author recommends in this book are ones that the author personally likes. You need to do your own research to find the ones that are best for you.

For information about permission to reproduce selections from this book, write to Permissions, Countryman Press, 500 Fifth Avenue, New York, NY 10110

For information about special discounts for bulk purchases, please contact W. W. Norton Special Sales at specialsales@wwnorton.com or 800-233-4830

Manufacturing by Lakeside Book Company
Production manager: Devon Zahn

Countryman Press
www.countrymanpress.com

An imprint of W. W. Norton & Company, Inc.
500 Fifth Avenue, New York, NY 10110
www.wwnorton.com

978-1-68268-892-2

10 9 8 7 6 5 4 3 2 1

To my wonderful husband, Justin

CONTENTS

INTRODUCTION

Like most kids, I couldn't wait for summer vacation. My dad was in the Air Force, and we moved around quite a lot, but no matter where I was in the world, for one month, I got to live with my grandmother in Arkansas.

Those Arkansas summers felt like magic. She lived in a small two-bedroom apartment, and that second bedroom always felt like home. We'd marathon old movie musicals, eat dessert first, go on long walks, and I even got to work with her.

She worked at the Arkansas Rice Depot, a hunger relief organization. Specifically, she worked with the Food For Kids program and delivered food all over the state in a Sprinter van. Arkansas ranks fourth in the nation for childhood hunger, and nearly one in four children face food hardship.

The Food For Kids program provided schools with food for meal-programs, and the backpack program whereby easy-to-prepare foods, such as oatmeal, granola bars, canned soup, mac and cheese, and PB&J, were discreetly sent home in backpacks for students on a weekly or daily basis.

During the summer, she'd plot all her routes for the week across the state, and we'd wake up at five a.m. to try to beat the morning traffic. When we got to Rice Depot, the van was loaded and ready to go. Then, we'd set off on an adventure.

I got an intimate look at my home state from the passenger-side window. We explored all sorts of back roads, the foothills of the Ozark Mountains, and tried to find small towns with the best names—my personal favorite being Possum Grape. We played the Patsy Cline CD until it broke, rode past miles of rice fields, and stopped at small-town diners for mashed potatoes and hand pies.

When we'd reach a school on the list, my grandmother would grab her clipboard and call out how many cases of each type of food were to be dropped off. I would ferret my way into the van and hand the cases to someone at the school who'd load them onto a dolly. Once we finished the drop, we'd jump back in the van and head to the next school until the van was empty. Then, we'd return home and prepare to do the same thing the next day.

My grandmother passed away in 2017, but spending those summers with her remains one of my favorite childhood memories. She instilled my love for musical theatre, for always ordering dessert, and taught me about the importance of community, politics, and how all of that plays into issues such as income inequality and hunger.

According to the USDA, more than 34 million people, including 9 million children, are food insecure in the United States. We could feed them all with what we throw away and *still* have food leftover—so . . . why don't we?

I'm going to do a little math. I love math, but if numbers aren't your particular cup of tea, feel free to skip the equations and head straight to the next section.

The Math

Feeding America reports the average meal weighs 1.2 pounds. Assuming three meals a day, that's 3.6 pounds of food, but for the sake of this example, let's round to 4.

34,000,000 people are experiencing food insecurity × 4 pounds of food = 136,000,000 pounds of food.

136,000,000 pounds of food a day × 365 = 49,640,000,000 pounds of food each year. For this example, let's round to an even 50 billion.

In the United States, we waste 40 percent of all our food. In 2021, ReFED estimated that 80 million TONS of food were wasted.

1 ton = 2,000 pounds

80,000,000 × 2,000 = 160,000,000,000 pounds

With 160 billion pounds of food wasted, there is an accompanying wastage of:

- 22.4 trillion gallons of water
- 380 million metric tons of CO_2e
- $444 billion

So, with the 160 billion pounds of food wasted, we could easily cover the 50 billion pounds needed to feed every person facing food insecurity, and we'd still have 110 billion pounds leftover.

The Takeaway

I think the most interesting part of the ReFED's research is that more than half of all our food waste comes from the residential sector, meaning our very own kitchens.

- Residential: 43.6 million tons—54.5%
- Farm (produce only): 13.5 million tons—16.9%
- Foodservice: 12.8 million tons—16%
- Manufacturing: 7.02 million tons—8.8%
- Retail: 3.01 million tons—3.8%

In low-income areas, waste usually occurs unintentionally. It happens on the farm or during storage and distribution. In wealthier regions, food waste occurs further along the supply chain, such as with retailers and consumers.

In the United States, retailers often reject food based on superficial characteristics, such as a minor blemish or a scar, if it's a little too big or small or slightly misshapen.

Yes, we have beauty standards for our food. Produce with the slightest imperfection, even one that has no bearing on flavor, freshness, or quality, will be rejected from grocery store shelves.

For instance, here's an illustration of a USDA card for strawberries. The top row is considered acceptable, but the bottom two rows are deemed unacceptable due to their shape, no matter how delicious they may be.

Sometimes, this less-than-perfect produce makes it to a food bank or becomes livestock feed, but arranging transportation can be expensive or prohibitive due to time constraints. More often than not, it's left in the field to rot or carted to the landfill.

You might think, *Well, who cares if my food scraps go to a landfill; won't they just biodegrade?* But get this: When food or organic matter is sent to a landfill, it doesn't really decompose because landfills are designed for storage, not decomposition. And in this big storage bin of trash, trapped organic matter—such as your food scraps—releases methane. Methane is around 30 times more potent than carbon dioxide. When I say more potent, I mean it hangs out in the atmosphere longer and has a more significant warming effect. And 16 percent of all methane emissions in the United States come from landfills.

This, of course, doesn't even account for all the energy, resources, and money put into growing, processing, packaging, and transporting it.

Producing uneaten food also means squandering valuable resources, such as seeds, water, energy, land, fertilizer, and the time and effort of people who worked to grow and harvest it, increasing emissions throughout the entire food production and distribution process.

All of this makes food waste, if it were a country, the third-largest emitter of greenhouse gases behind the United States and China.

Beyond the climate aspect, we haven't even brushed the financial aspect. According to the USDA, the average American family of four loses at least $1,500 annually to uneaten food.

The food waste documentary *Just Eat It* reveals that households were wasting between 15 and 25 percent of their purchased food. It's like walking out of a grocery store with four bags of food, dropping one in the parking lot, and leaving it behind.

Our food waste happens for several reasons:

- Not going into the grocery store with a plan
- Not understanding how to store and preserve produce properly
- Misunderstanding best-by, sell-by, and use-by dates
- Not knowing how to use all parts and get the most out of produce

For instance, fresh broccoli costs $1.99 per pound at my local grocery store. Most households in the United States cut off the stalk and eat only the florets. Right there, you're paying an extra dollar for something you're throwing away, and the stalk is delicious if you know how to use it (see page 129).

Throughout this book, we'll explore my top tips to prevent food waste in your home because it will save you money and was cited as the NUMBER ONE solution to reducing greenhouse gas emissions, according to Project Drawdown in 2022.

From my experience, there are three key areas in which you can prevent food waste in your home. So, I wanted to create an easy and approachable handbook to help you solve these three problems. The goal of this book is to help make your kitchen routines both *manageable* and *enjoyable*! By incorporating these three essential practices, you can simplify your post-grocery-shopping routine, save time, and ensure that your food stays fresh and accessible.

First, we'll cover how to set yourself up for success by prepping and planning with ease. Then, we'll talk about how to store your produce for maximum efficiency and finish up with some of my favorite recipes and ways to utilize your produce even after it's passed its prime.

Now, the second most impactful swap, according to Project Drawdown, is adopting a plant-rich diet. Animal agriculture contributes significantly to greenhouse gas emissions, and choosing more plant-based foods—fruits, veggies, legumes, etc.—significantly lowers your carbon footprint; requires less land, water, and energy; and helps preserve biodiversity by reducing deforestation and habitat loss. So, all of the recipes provided in this book will also be plant-based.[*]

Two impactful swaps, one delicious book. What could be better than that?

---

[*] However, it would be imprudent to ignore that most households in the United States consume animal products. Acknowledging this, I think it is important to address the issue of food waste because it comes with the absolute highest price tag in both an economical and ecological sense. If it's going to be purchased, the least that can be done is to ensure not a bit goes to waste!

CHAPTER 1

GROCERY PREP AND MEAL PLANNING

If you want to avoid food waste, you need to set yourself up for success. And that happens before you click order, head to the farmers' market, or even step foot inside a grocery store. In this chapter, we're going to examine our habits, practice intentional meal planning, and sustainable shopping practices.

Examining our current shopping and eating habits is crucial because there's often a disconnect between who we want to be and who we actually are. If we can recognize that gap, we can shift our shopping habits and behaviors and bring those together. This not only creates a more conscious and fulfilling relationship with food, it also allows us to save money and reduce waste.

Grocery stores use some sneaky psychological tricks to encourage you to spend more money and buy more food than you need. One way they do this is through abundance. They create appealing displays that overflow with food, which stimulates our senses, can trigger cravings, and encourages you to buy more. They also like to put staples, such as milk and bread, at the back of the store. This often forces you to walk through aisles of tempting snack foods complete with eye-catching, colorful graphics and promotional offers that make them difficult to resist. And when you end up buying things you don't need, the likelihood that they will go to waste rises. An effective way to reduce buying too much at the store is to create a meal plan and stick to it.

Even if meal planning is your least favorite chore, I've created several strategies to help you plan and get meals on the table fast. By understanding your schedule, energy levels, and preferred cooking times, we can develop a plan that allows you freedom and suits your current needs. Once you actually get to the grocery store, we'll look at a few easy swaps that will make your trips more intentional and eco-friendly.

The average American goes to the grocery store at least once a week, so many of these small swaps will add up to a major impact over a year and beyond!

1. Get to Know Your Habits

How well do you know yourself and your eating habits? I find there are two versions of myself. There's the aspirational version of myself and then the real-life version of myself.

The aspirational version of myself is filled with wonder, opportunity, and excitement. This idealized version of myself typically does the grocery shopping. I love her for her optimism, hope, and spontaneity, but boy, she gets me in trouble. She'll gleefully grab a gorgeous piece of produce that she's never tried before. Does she look up a recipe and see what other ingredients she has to make it work? Of course not—she's a dreamer, not a planner.

Aspirational Kathryn will decide she wants a salad and buy enough for the whole week. But did she check the weather forecast and see that the high will be 35°F by tomorrow? Of course not.

I can't speak for you, but I'm a soup girl when it dips below 40°F. If I'd only checked the weather, I could have gone with a kale-based salad, which easily could double into a delicious Tuscan white bean and kale soup when the weather took a turn. So, real-life Kathryn is often stuck dealing with aspirational Kathryn's poor choices. Even though those poor choices were made with the best of intentions.

When you shop without understanding your own eating habits, it can lead to tons of food waste. But if you go into the grocery store knowing exactly what food will suit your needs, you're much less likely to end up throwing out that poor rutabaga you didn't know what to do with, or the spinach that went bad before you could make a salad. So, think about what kind of shopper you are and how you could best shop to fit your own lifestyle and eating habits.

What Kind of Shopper Are You?

After studying my and others' shopping patterns, I've identified the three main types of shoppers. You might be one, two, or hit the trifecta and be all three—like me! Take the quiz and find out whether you're a dreamer, achiever, or seeker.

INSTRUCTIONS: *For each question, choose the option that best represents your grocery-shopping and meal-planning habits. Be honest in your answers to get the most accurate results. At the end of the quiz, tally up your answers and see which personality type best describes your shopping style!*

1. When you go grocery shopping, what is your approach to buying ingredients?

    a. I love exploring new ingredients and buy them without a specific plan.

    b. I tend to buy ingredients for elaborate meals that require a lot of time and effort.

    c. I often buy more ingredients than I can realistically use before they spoil.

    d. I plan my meals in advance and buy ingredients accordingly.

2. How often do you find yourself not using all the ingredients you bought before they go bad?

    a. Frequently. I buy things on a whim and struggle to use them all.

    b. Occasionally. I often overestimate my energy and time available for cooking.

c. Quite often. I tend to buy more food than I can consume before it spoils.

d. Rarely. I plan my meals carefully and use ingredients efficiently.

3. How well do your grocery shopping habits align with your lifestyle and cooking routine?

a. Not very well. I'm more of a spontaneous cook and adapt my plans based on my mood.

b. Not well at all. I often buy ingredients that require more time and effort than I can give.

c. Not too well. I often overestimate the amount of food I can realistically consume.

d. Very well. I carefully consider my lifestyle and cooking routine when planning my groceries.

4. How often do you end up ordering takeout or eating out?

a. Frequently. I enjoy trying different cuisines and restaurants.

b. Quite often. I often feel too exhausted to prepare the elaborate meals I desire.

c. Occasionally. Sometimes I order food to prevent ingredients from going to waste.

d. Rarely. I prioritize cooking at home and have a good balance of energy and motivation.

Now, let's tally up your answers!

Mostly As: Congratulations, you are a Dreamer! You love the excitement of discovering new ingredients and being spontaneous in the kitchen. Your creativity shines through your diverse grocery shopping, even if it sometimes leads to a lack of meal plans.

Mostly Bs: Congratulations, you are an Achiever! Your ambition leads you to buy ingredients for elaborate meals, but you may find it challenging to execute these plans due to exhaustion after work. Remember to find a balance that aligns with your energy levels.

Mostly Cs: Congratulations, you are a Seeker! Your enthusiasm for food often leads you to buy more ingredients than you can realistically consume before they spoil. Focus on better meal planning and portion control to reduce food waste.

Mostly Ds: Congratulations, you are a Planner! Your organized approach to grocery shopping and meal planning ensures that you make the most of your ingredients and avoid food waste. Keep up the great work!

THE DREAMER

You might be a dreamer if you go to the grocery store and are seduced by beautiful packaging, you want to try all sorts of new ingredients but have no idea if you'll actually like them, or you buy things without any kind of plan.

If I sound like I'm trying to dissuade you from trying new things, I'm not! I love trying new things. In fact, I used to have a pantry FULL of things I wanted to try. But I never had any follow-through. I'd buy it in the store without a plan to use it, and it would clutter up my pantry as it got passed over for my tried-and-true staple recipes and ingredients.

So, my little dreamer, if you too want to try new things and avoid falling into my trap of a full pantry, but nothing to eat—here are my top three tips:

Try with a friend who likes and uses that product

When I lived in California, one of my friends LOVED papaya, which I had never tried. I was supercurious so when I saw a good-looking one, I tossed it in the cart. Now, papayas are a big fruit, so that's a *big* commitment to buying something I'd never tasted.

The intelligent thing would have been to try it at her house, in a fruit cup at a café, or at a market stall that lets you sample before you buy. Instead, I just wheeled my giant papaya home, grabbed a spoonful, and realized I do not like papaya.

Thankfully, I gave it to my friend, who ate the rest. I'd like to tell you that was the first and only time I made that mistake, but we all know that's not true.

Learn from my wasteful mistakes and save lots of resources and money in the process.

Shop the bulk and sample section

See whether the product you want to try is available in the bulk section. There, you can pay per pound and get a single serving to try.

I've noticed more single-serving samples in the grocery store. I recently bought a handful of packets from the protein powder section. I've been hunting for one that doesn't taste like baby powder or hurt my stomach. Who would've thought that would be such an arduous quest?

While I don't love the single-serving idea from a packaging standpoint, it is far less wasteful (and way cheaper!) than buying a big tub and realizing that you don't like it at all.

Allow yourself a treat, but do it with a plan

If trying new things at the grocery store brings you immense joy, I don't want to stop you. I just want to get you into the habit of creating a plan and a routine.

The next time you're at the store, and you see a new ingredient, write it down in your grocery list for the *next time* you're shopping. Go home and find a recipe to incorporate this new ingredient. Double-check what the recipe calls for to confirm what you already have or need to buy. Then, enjoy your new discovery.

THE ACHIEVER

You might be an achiever if you shop in a way that doesn't fit your lifestyle. Maybe you dream of making elaborate, time-consuming recipes, but after work, you're too tired to spend three hours in the kitchen.

Maybe you're like me and plan to make kale salads for every meal, only to realize you're really not that crazy about kale. The aspirational version of yourself loves kale, but the actual real-life version of yourself would rather have butter lettuce.

I've always had a disconnect between the person I think I am and the person I actually am. Real Kathryn versus Idealized Kathryn. And that, *that*, gets me into trouble. In my mind, I'm excellent at gardening, love yoga, spend three hours a day in the kitchen, and for some reason dress to the nines a few times a month. In real life, I am a terrible gardener, I'd much rather be at a dance class, am lucky to spend an hour in the kitchen, and live at the theater where I'm always in dance clothes. So, why do I have so many formal dresses? I don't know. And when shopping, I have to remember, I'm shopping for Real Kathryn, not Idealized Kathryn.

Real Kathryn needs quick, high-protein snacks. She needs easy-to-prep and portable food, and if I don't have it—that means I'm far more likely to wind up ordering takeout or eating out.

While there's nothing wrong with either of those options, it can be expensive and quite wasteful with all of that takeout packaging. And if I'm ordering takeout, all those idealized groceries— they are languishing away in the fridge.

If you're an achiever, sit down with your schedule and have an honest heart-to-heart with yourself about what you *really* need. Pay close attention to the foods you consistently reach for, and WHY you're reaching for them.

- Is it a quick meal you can make in under 30 minutes? A sandwich
- Is it something you're always craving? Also a sandwich
- Does it require little to no cleanup? Have I mentioned I like sandwiches?
- Does it make a bunch of leftovers you love to eat? Chili

I ate a peanut butter and jelly sandwich every day for school from kindergarten till I graduated. However, in all honesty, I briefly visited the baked potato bar a few times in the fifth grade.

Sandwiches are my comfort food, but you can choose whatever food works for you. And it's okay if some of the reasonings don't make sense. For instance, I enjoy grapes socially. If someone is coming over for a movie night or I'm going over to a friend's house for a game night, I always bring grapes. I love them, but there's nothing in the world that could compel me to eat grapes by myself. I don't know why, but grapes are only good in groups. Does it make sense? No. Does it have to? Also no. You just have to know yourself and shop accordingly. Aspirational Kathryn would love to buy grapes for herself, but real-life Kathryn knows only to buy them for a social engagement.

Now, that you've identified why you buy things, what you

need, and what works for your schedule—take a month or two to get into a good routine. Then, you can start trying to make mealtime even more eco-friendly by reducing packaging waste and incorporating more plant-based options.

Maybe you like to make a big batch of soup that you can eat throughout the week. Could you make a veggie lentil soup? Could you make a vegetarian chili? Could you cook the dried beans in a slow cooker? (*Dried beans are a total bargain, and have reduced packaging.*)

This slow approach over time should allow you to make changes that will stick.

THE SEEKER

You might be a seeker if you buy more food than you or your family can eat. I was guilty of this when I had one of those massive double-door fridges. I would buy groceries to fill the fridge instead of buying what I need.

My fridge experiences ranged from a single shelf in actor housing to a mini-fridge in a tiny home. I always filled and utilized every square inch of space, so when I moved to a new apartment with a large French-door fridge, I did what I always did—I filled it.

Like many people, my consumer habits were linked to filling space simply because it's empty. And when we fill space without purpose, it leads to clutter. Very rarely are we filling space with things we actually use and love.

When I lived in a tiny home (325 square feet), I was so strict about what I brought into the house, but when I moved to a larger apartment (900 square feet and the one with the offending fridge), I became less strict because I had more space. Unsurprisingly this resulted in more clutter because we adapt to our space, whether that's closet space, empty drawers, cupboards, or fridges. I could write a whole 'nother book on sustainable decluttering and embracing empty space but, right now, I have to go back to the fridge.

My double-decker fridge had 26 cubic feet of space. According to my local appliance shop, a 26-cubic-foot fridge is ideal for a family of five. Being a family of two, no wonder food would go bad on us. We were overstocked, and things were constantly being shoved to the back of the fridge. We would lose track of things we couldn't see, resulting in food waste.

Eventually, I learned to embrace the empty space and how to organize everything properly. There's a whole section for tips on organizing your fridge (see page 62), so in this section, I want to focus on how to embrace buying less.

You must go into the store with a plan. There are three methods of planning, and I detail all of them on page 4. But for the seeker, the easiest piece of advice I can give you is to buy food for one less meal than you think you need.

I always worry about running out of food, and this shows up in two ways. One, I tend to overbuy food. After meticulously going through my grocery list, I go rogue and throw random things in the cart *"just in case."* The second way this manifests is that I am afraid to finish things. I am afraid to eat the last few bites, just in case I need it for some other hypothetical reason. Of course, this results in those last few bites going bad.

I consistently have to remind myself that more food exists. If I run out of an item, I can buy more. If I need another ingredient or another meal, I can buy more. I do not need to buy everything right now because I can always go back to the store and *buy more*.

When shopping, try to buy for one fewer meal than you think

you need. Each week, I roughly (very roughly—planning is not my strong suit) plan five breakfasts, five lunches, and five dinners. Let's say my dinner looks like tacos, pasta, pizza, burgers, and stir-fry. Before I go shopping, I cross one of those meals off of my list *because—*

Without fail, every week, at least one of these things happens:

- I get invited over to friends for dinner.
- I will have a late lunch and not feel up to a big meal.
- One of those meals will make more leftovers than expected.

So, when I'm at the grocery store and tempted to buy more food than I actually need, I always remind myself that the grocery store will be there later, and if I need more food, I can always go back.

Another way we reduced food waste was by downsizing our fridge. I don't necessarily recommend this tip unless you're truly in need of a fridge, but we were. We recently moved into an *adorable,* modestly sized historic home. Which came with a very *adorable,* modestly sized kitchen. There are nine kitchen cabinets, no pantry, and the biggest fridge we could accommodate would fit in most RVs. And I couldn't be happier. I love our petite fridge. I don't know if it's weird to name your fridge, but I call her Juliette. She can easily fit a week's worth of groceries, and it's organized to perfection. Everything can be seen, so everything gets eaten.

$2.$ Meal Plan

Are you good at planning? I'm not. Well, at least not meal planning. I find meal planning to be futile. But like it or not, meal planning is a perfect way to ensure that you'll use all of the food you buy, and ideally, before it goes bad. For example, if you meal plan, you can make sure to use veggies that will go bad early in the week, or you can buy a new kind of produce with more purpose, knowing that you'll learn how to use it in a recipe you found ahead of time. Whatever meal planning looks like for you, I encourage you to prepare for the grocery store in some way!

What Kind of Meal Planning Works for You?

Meal planning in the traditional sense is completely and utterly lost on me. Without a doubt, if I declared Tuesday lasagna day, I would crave literally anything, *anything,* other than lasagna. Maybe to you, laying out your meals is a blessing. Maybe you love not having to think about what's for dinner. Or maybe you love the spontaneity that comes from having creative freedom and getting to cook what you're in the mood for.

If you're looking for your ideal meal-planning style, take this quiz to see which meal plan might be right for you.

INSTRUCTIONS: *For each question, choose the option that best represents your meal planning preferences. Be honest in your answers to get the most accurate results. At the end of the quiz, tally up your answers and see which personality type best describes your meal-planning style!*

1. How do you prefer to approach meal planning?

a. I enjoy having a structured plan, knowing exactly what I'll eat each day.

b. I like to have a loose plan with some flexibility to decide my meals on the go.

c. I prefer to go with the flow and experiment with different dishes spontaneously.

2. How important is it for you to have a set schedule for specific meals?

a. Very important. I keep a tight calendar designating certain days for specific meals, themes, times, and events.

b. Moderately important. I prefer having a rough idea but with room for changes.

c. Not important at all. I prefer deciding my meals spontaneously, based on my mood.

3. How comfortable are you with improvising in the kitchen?

a. Not comfortable. I prefer following recipes and sticking to a plan.

b. Moderately comfortable. I can make adjustments but within certain limits.

c. Very comfortable. I enjoy experimenting and creating new dishes on the spot.

4. How do you handle leftovers when meal planning?

a. I have a plan to ensure all leftovers are incorporated into future meals.

b. I'm open to using leftovers creatively but don't rely on them heavily.

c. I'm not great at incorporating leftovers and can let food go to waste.

Now, let's tally up your answers!

Mostly As: Congratulations, you are a Traditional Meal Planner! You thrive on structure and enjoy having set meal plans. You appreciate the consistency and knowing exactly what to expect on specific days or meals.

Mostly Bs: Congratulations, you are a Five-Minute Meal Planner! You like to have a loose plan with room for flexibility. You appreciate the opportunity to decide your meals based on your mood or circumstances while still having some level of organization.

Mostly Cs: Congratulations, you are a No-Plan Planner! You love the freedom and spontaneity of cooking without strict meal plans. Your culinary knowledge allows you to experiment and create dishes on the spot. However, be mindful of potential food waste and find creative ways to utilize ingredients effectively.

THE TRADITIONAL MEAL PLAN

The Traditional Meal Plan involves sitting down before grocery shopping, taking inventory of what you have, and planning exactly what you're going to eat every day. Then, you make a list and take it to the grocery store. You make and eat exactly what you have planned.

Pros
- Easily account for everything you buy and make sure nothing goes to waste
- Avoid decision fatigue
- Most streamlined way to get food on the table

Cons

- Provides very little flexibility
- Most time-consuming to plan

1. Set a Schedule: Choose a specific day and time each week to dedicate to meal planning. This consistency will make it easier to stick to the routine.

2. Assess Your Needs: Consider such factors as dietary preferences, health goals, budget, and the number of meals you need to plan for, like breakfast, lunch, dinner, and snacks.

3. Gather Recipes: Look for recipe inspiration from cookbooks, online sources, or family favorites. Aim for a variety of meals to keep things interesting and include a balance of proteins, vegetables, grains, and other food groups.

4. Plan Your Meals: Take a weekly calendar or a meal-planning app and assign specific recipes to each day. Consider any time constraints or special events that may impact your meal choices.

5. Make a Shopping List: Based on your planned meals, create a detailed shopping list. Check your pantry and fridge for any items you already have, and prioritize what you need to buy. This will help you avoid unnecessary purchases and reduce food waste.

6. Shop with Purpose: Head to the grocery store or shop online with your list in hand. Stick to your planned items as much as possible, but remain open to substitutes, if necessary.

7. Prep Ahead: If you have time, consider prepping some ingredients in advance, such as chopping vegetables or marinating proteins. This can save time during busy weekdays.

8. Stay Flexible: It's okay if your plans change during the week. Be adaptable and willing to adjust meals if needed. Leftovers can also serve as convenient meals.

9. Repeat and Reflect: Repeat the meal-planning process each week, adjusting as necessary. Take note of what worked well and what didn't to refine your future meal plans.

THE 5-MINUTE MEAL PLAN

The 5-minute meal plan involves taking stock of what you have and planning meals based on flavor profile rather than strict recipes. You'll pick three or four flavor profiles you enjoy and consistently cook from that style and region. This allows you a lot more freedom and flexibility. Plus, you can easily incorporate more seasonal produce, such as a tomato galette during the summer, vs a butternut squash galette during the fall.

The key to really making this plan work is having a stocked pantry and spice rack with everything you'll need. And while I've personally narrowed my cooking options down to three to four flavor profiles, that doesn't mean I don't enjoy other cuisines. For instance, I don't cook a lot of Indian or Thai food. I didn't grow up eating or making those recipes with my family. So, I prefer to enjoy and support my local restaurants specializing in that cuisine.

Pros
- Takes only five minutes
- Allows for a lot of flexibility based on mood and preference
- Stretches creativity and culinary exploration

Cons
- Could cause decision fatigue
- Less structured—if you like cooking from specific recipes rather than based on feeling, you might find this more challenging
- Limited variety

1. Identify Flavor Profiles: Start by choosing three or four core flavor profiles that you enjoy and typically crave during the week. For example, you might like American, Mexican, Greek, Indian, or Italian foods. Each flavor profile typically includes a combination of spices, herbs, and ingredients that are characteristic of that cuisine.

2. Research Ingredients: Explore recipes or online resources that align with your chosen flavor profiles, and make a list of common ingredients used in those dishes. You want to be familiar with common ingredients and how you can enhance them with different spices, herbs, and sauces based on your selected flavor profile. So, if you like chickpeas, you could use those to create hummus or falafels, but you could also use that ingredient for chana masala.

3. Pick Your Core Dishes: Once you've selected your flavor profiles, pinpoint at least five dishes you enjoy in every category. If you've chosen Italian food you might have spaghetti with red sauce, homemade pizza, eggplant parmesan, lasagna, and fettuccine Alfredo. I keep a list of all my favorite meals organized by flavor profile and look for where things overlap.

4. Look for the Overlap: A key ingredient in eggplant parmesan is eggplant, so if eggplant is in season and you also have Greek food for one of your core flavor profiles, you might want to add moussaka to your reference sheet. If you have a French flavor profile, consider making ratatouille. Alternatively, the overlap can also happen by season. For example, potpie is on my list of core dishes. I often make it with navy beans, but sub out the produce depending on what's in season. During the summer I'll add zucchini, summer squash, and corn, but during the winter, I use heartier root vegetables, such as carrots, potatoes, and onions.

5. Stock the Pantry: Because you have more flexibility with your proteins and produce, always keep sauces and seasonings that enhance the flavor profiles you've selected. Here's a rough idea of what you might want to keep on hand, depending on your selected cuisines.

AMERICAN FOOD

Pantry Staples: Flour, sugar, butter, milk, bread crumbs, canned beans, canned tomatoes

Herbs and Spices: Parsley, rosemary, paprika, chili powder, garlic powder, onion powder, cayenne pepper, dried oregano, dried thyme

Sauces: Barbecue sauce, ketchup, mustard, hot sauce, Worcestershire sauce, ranch dressing

CHINESE FOOD

Pantry Staples: Rice, noodles, tofu, cornstarch

Herbs and Spices: Green onions, ginger, garlic, star anise, Chinese five-spice powder, Sichuan peppercorns, sesame seeds

Sauces: Soy sauce, oyster sauce, hoisin sauce, rice vinegar, sesame oil, chili sauce

FRENCH FOOD

Pantry Staples: Butter, flour, sugar, salt, pepper, olive oil, wine, vegetable stock

Herbs and Spices: Chives, basil, thyme, rosemary, parsley, tarragon, bay leaves

Sauces: Red and white wine vinegar, Dijon mustard

GREEK FOOD

Pantry Staples: Olive oil, lemon juice, garlic, onions, tomatoes, olives, yogurt

Herbs and Spices: Mint, parsley, oregano, thyme, dill

Sauces: Tzatziki sauce, lemon-oregano dressing, tahini

MEXICAN FOOD

Pantry Staples: Tortillas, rice, black beans, canned tomatoes, chipotle peppers, canned chilies, canned corn, avocado

Herbs and Spices: Cilantro, chili powder, cumin, paprika, oregano, coriander

Sauces: Salsa, mole sauce, enchilada sauce

ITALIAN FOOD

Pantry Staples: Pasta, olive oil, tomatoes (canned or fresh), garlic, onions

Herbs and Spices: Parsley, basil, oregano, basil, thyme, rosemary

Sauces: Marinara sauce, pesto sauce, balsamic glaze

Please note that this is a very general overview meant for inspiration. Specific ingredients can vary based on regional variations and personal preferences within each cuisine.

6. Think about Texture: Consider the textures and complementary ingredients that enhance your chosen flavors. Think of having something crunchy, creamy, or chewy and how all of those elements play together.

7. Experiment and Adapt: Stay open to new ingredients or variations as you shop. If you come across an ingredient that fits within your flavor profiles but wasn't on your original list, feel free to adapt and try it out.

THE NO-PLAN MEAL PLAN

When I say *no plan*, there are still about 30 seconds of planning involved. But all you have to do is head to your fridge and see what perishables you have left and need to eat first. Then, you can head to the store without even creating a list. It's practical and flexible, but also the most likely to end with food waste.

Pros
- Complete flexibility and spontaneity
- Takes less than five minutes
- Easy to take advantage of sales and seasonality

Cons
- Very little organization
- Impulse purchases and accidental overbuying
- Could result in more food waste than the other two options

1. Assess Your Kitchen: Before heading to the grocery store, take a quick inventory of what you already have in your pantry, refrigerator, and freezer. This will give you an idea of what ingredients you can work with and what items you need to restock.

2. Choose Proteins: Start by selecting four protein sources that can serve as the foundation for your meals. Subtract one protein source for every protein source already in your fridge. Some of my favorite options are fried tofu, smoked tofu, black beans, seitan, and veggie burger patties. Also, consider the versatility and cooking times of each protein to make meal preparation easier. Pick at least one thing that cooks quickly or requires no cooking at all for a night when you're tired or busy.

3. Select Fresh Produce: Explore the produce section and choose a variety of four fruits and six vegetables that are in season or on sale. Subtract one fruit or veg for each one you already have in your fridge. Opt for a mix of colors and textures to ensure a well-rounded nutritional intake. This will allow you to incorporate a range of flavors into your meals.

4. Consider Staples and Pantry Items: Think about staple items that can round out your meals. These could include grains (rice, pasta, quinoa), canned goods (beans, tomatoes), condiments (sauces, spices), and any other pantry essentials you regularly use. These items can help create flavor profiles and add depth to your meals.

5. Create Meal Combos: As you shop, mentally note potential meal combinations based on the items you've selected. Think about pairing the protein with different vegetables, grains, and sauces to create various flavor profiles. For example, chicken fried tofu with roasted veggies and baked beans or tofu stir-fry with rice noodles and a ginger carrot sauce.

6. Adapt as You Go: Remain flexible and adaptable during the shopping process. If you come across a new ingredient or special offer that sparks inspiration, don't hesitate to adjust your meal plan on the spot. This allows for spontaneity and encourages culinary experimentation.

Pro Tip: *For any meal plan, make sure you don't go to the grocery store hungry! I know it's been said 1,000 times. We all know we aren't supposed to do it, but inevitably we still do. When I do, I always wind up with extra, random items—usually snacks. So, grab a snack before you go, or treat yourself to a bite out before you hit the store.*

3. BYOB/Bring Reusable Bags

The first, and maybe the easiest way to shop with intention is to come prepared. While food waste has always been my biggest waste-reducing passion, single-use plastics have to be a very close second. Using a reusable bag at the grocery store is a simple, easy, and impactful choice.

Single-use plastic bags are made of polyethylene. They're thin pieces of plastic that are very difficult to recycle and have a very low, practically nonexistent recycling rate. According to Environment America, Americans use more than 100 billion plastic bags each year. That adds up to 300 bags per person *per year*. These bags are used for an average of 12 minutes, but the life expectancy of a single-use plastic bag is more than 1,000 years. When they do "break down," they just break apart into teeny tiny particles—they never really go away.

All that being said, I think most of us know we *should* bring our reusable bags to the grocery store. But it can sometimes be a challenge to actually remember them. So, here are some tips on how to remember them.

First, try getting on a schedule. Take a look at your regular routines and see whether there's a pattern. Do you usually pass by the grocery store on certain days while heading home from work? Do you prefer to shop on weeknights or weekends? Knowing when you'll be going to the store can help you remember to have your bags with you. You can even make a schedule for yourself, dedicating specific days of the week to grocery shopping.

Another tip is to place your bags under your keys once you bring your groceries in. That way, the next morning, when you grab your keys, you'll remember to grab your bags, too. If you do a lot of walking, there are even bags available that clip onto your keyring, so you'll always be prepared wherever you go. It may be just one bag, but if you're on foot, you typically won't need more than one or two.

And when you're ready to graduate, grab a few reusable produce bags and/or a bread bag, so you can cut out all sorts of single-use plastics at the store. If you want a more in-depth look at reducing single-use plastics and all sorts of household waste, I highly recommend my first book, *101 Ways to Go Zero Waste*.

4. Minimize Packaging

I used to be very strict about plastic and packaging. I even ran a two-year experiment to see just how little trash I could produce, and documented that journey on my blog and through social media. I eschewed plastic for health reasons as well as environmental reasons. But when COVID-19 hit, I started reevaluating my relationship with plastic. All of the bulk bins at my local supermarket were plastic-wrapped shut. Cafés stopped accepting cups from home, and cities that had plastic bag bans for years were reversing their stance when so little was known about the transmission of the disease.

It was an odd experience. For about five years, before the pandemic, I ate only what I could get from a bulk bin. Being in the San Francisco area, I had a lot of variety, but I still went two years without blueberries, my favorite fruit. Thankfully, in 2017, a farmer opened a stand at my local farmers' market, and I could buy them in my own container. That sort of dedication is . . . admirable? Slightly unhinged? Both? You can decide. However, I don't think I'd ever put myself through that again.

When I first started grocery shopping again during the pandemic, I would only buy the exact products that I could get from the bulk bins. For instance, I would buy a particular snack mix from the bins. But, after having snack mix for five years instead of potato chips—I really just wanted some potato chips. At the end of the day, I realized a plastic bag for snack mix is the exact same as a plastic bag for potato chips. I might as well just buy what I actually want.

This lead me to my current ethos—moderation. There are so

many things that I do to be more sustainable that I'm not going to worry about a few groceries that come in plastic. While there are still some things I would never buy in plastic from a health perspective, such as oils, peanut butter, and so on, I don't let plastic scare me away anymore or dictate all of my purchasing decisions. Instead, I try to focus on the bigger picture, which I hope you can gather from this whole book.

Even though I've let go of my dogmatism, I still think reducing plastic is good and important. I now go for about a 60/40 split. I want 60 percent of my cart to be unpackaged. Then, 20 percent can be minimally packaged staples and ingredients, such as pasta in a box, rice, quinoa, or flour. Then the other 20 percent is convenience-focused to help me get meals on the table fast or treats like salsa, a new salad dressing, crackers, tofu, plant milk, or even a bag of potato chips.

When I was really strict about my plastic packaging, I would make all of those products myself, and that was very time consuming. It's great not having to make salsa every time I want it, and I'm still able to reduce tons of plastic packaging with the 60/40 mentality. So, here are a few things I keep in mind when shopping:

BYOB: As we talked about above, bringing your own bags to the grocery store is an easy way to reduce plastic waste. Consider adding some produce bags to your arsenal, and if you're shopping at a farmers' market or at a co-op, consider bringing some extra containers for such things as berries or bulk goods.

Shop the perimeter: Everyone typically recommends shopping the perimeter from a health perspective, but it's generally also a lot better in terms of packaging. Fresh produce, such as fruits and vegetables, are often sold loose or in bulk. You can also normally get unpackaged or minimally packaged products, such as bread and pastries, from bakery and deli sections.

Plant forward: If you're eating a plant-forward diet, this will also reduce packaging because so many fruits and veggies can be bought loose in the produce section. According to the Harvard Healthy Eating Plate, at least half of our plates should be fruits or vegetables, and one-quarter should be whole grains. Eating a colorful plant-based diet means lots of veggies and legumes, which are often some of the cheapest foods.

Bulk bins: If you have access to bulk bins, it's a great way to reduce plastic packaging. Here's my guide to bringing your own container to your local zero-waste store, co-op, or health food store.

- Select reusable containers that are clean, dry, and suitable for storing bulk items. Mason jars, glass containers with lids, or reusable food storage bags (you can decant into your own jars at home) are popular options. Make sure your containers are easy to seal securely.
- Weigh your empty containers at the customer service desk or designated weighing station. Take note of the weight or get a sticker to indicate the tare weight, which is the weight of the container. This ensures that the cashier can deduct the weight of your container when you check out. (I like to do this on a note app on my phone)
- At the bulk aisle, locate the items you need and use a scoop or provided utensil to fill your containers. Be mindful of any specific instructions or guidelines for filling containers, such as using a funnel for powdery items. If you're unsure, don't hesitate to ask the store staff for assistance.
- Label your containers with the item's PLU (price lookup) code or any other identifying information. This will make it easier for the cashier to ring up your purchases.
- After filling your containers, securely seal them to prevent any spills or contamination.

In bulk: Shopping in bulk is similar to shopping from bulk bins, but instead of buying a small amount, you're just purchasing a large quantity in the same way the store is. This works well if you have a large family or eat a lot of certain items. Maybe you're a baker and go through a lot of flour or you eat a lot of rice. As long as you can get through all of the food without wasting it and you have the space, this is a great way to save money and reduce waste.

No single-use: One of the main ways I reduce the amount of packaging I bring home, even without shopping from the bulk aisle, is by avoiding single-serve products. Buy a larger tub of yogurt and put what you need in a bowl, or prep it in your own to-go cups. Buy a larger bag of chips and space it out how you need to. Single-serve comes at a premium cost, so this is another win for saving money and reducing waste.

Material mindful: While packaging isn't the sole dictator of what I buy, I am still very mindful of what materials I purchase. First and foremost, I try to reduce all packaging, especially plastic, and then look for things that can easily be recycled or composted as well as packaging that contains a lot of recycled content.

I buy some staples, such as tofu or chips, in plastic. I buy a lot of such things as cereal, flour, sugar, and oats in paper and paperboard that can be recycled. I opt for things in glass jars that I can upcycle and reuse, and I buy some staples, such as beans and veggies, in steel tins.

5. Understand Use-By, Best-By and Sell-By Dates

These dates can be very misleading and significantly contribute to food waste. The Natural Resources Defense Council estimates that confusion over date labeling is responsible for 20 percent of food waste in the United States. The USDA emphasizes that use-by, best-by, and sell-by dates are NOT federally regulated, *except* for infant formula.

"Best before" or "sell by" are indicators of *quality* rather than safety, and throwing food out after that date has passed is just unnecessary waste. Instead of relying solely on these dates, use your senses. How does it smell? How does it look? How does it taste?

Sell-by: This label is for retailers. It tells the store how long to display the product for sale. It's not a safety date.

Best-by: This is the date by which the product should be eaten for optimum quality, but it doesn't mean the product has gone bad. It's not a safety date.

Use-by: Last date recommended for use when the product is at peak quality. Not a safety date, except when used on infant formula. Products can go bad before and after these dates. It's not an exact science. The most reliable way to tell is with a smell and taste test.

To address this issue, organizations and initiatives are working to standardize and clarify date labeling practices. The Food

Date Labeling Act was introduced in the United States to establish a uniform national system for date labels.

Some retailers have also taken steps to reduce food waste by implementing policies such as selling misshapen produce or offering discounted prices for items close to their sell-by dates.

6. Look for Labels

When grocery shopping, it can be difficult to identify what a good and sustainable purchase is. A lot of packages might be green, have nature-y pictures, and use unregulated marketing words like "all-natural," "natural," "farm-fresh," "wholesome," and "artisanal." This is designed to make you think the product is healthy and sustainable.

When shopping, I look for certain certifications that are verified. While not perfect, these certifications can provide a way to identify products that meet specific environmental, social, and ethical standards. By looking for these certifications, you can align your purchasing decisions with your values and contribute to a more sustainable and responsible food system. Here are a few you may want to consider:

USDA Organic: USDA-certified organic foods are grown and processed according to federal guidelines addressing, among many factors, soil quality, animal-raising practices, pest and weed control, and use of additives. Organic producers rely on natural substances and physical, mechanical, or biologically based farming methods to the fullest extent possible.

Fair Trade: Fair Trade certification guarantees that products are sourced from producers who adhere to fair labor practices and receive fair prices for their goods. It promotes social sustainability and supports farmers in developing countries.

Rainforest Alliance Certified: Rainforest Alliance certification focuses on sustainable agriculture, promoting biodiversity conservation, ecosystem protection, and fair treatment of workers. It covers a range of products, including coffee, tea, cocoa, and bananas.

UTZ Certified: UTZ certification is now part of the Rainforest Alliance, and focuses on sustainable farming practices for such products as coffee, cocoa, and tea. It emphasizes environmental stewardship, social responsibility, and traceability throughout the supply chain.

Marine Stewardship Council (MSC): MSC certification ensures that seafood products come from sustainable fisheries that follow strict management practices to protect fish populations and minimize environmental impacts.

Certified Humane: Certified Humane certification focuses on animal welfare in livestock farming. It sets standards for the treatment of animals, including their living conditions, feed, and handling practices.

Demeter Biodynamic: Demeter Biodynamic certification goes beyond organic farming by incorporating holistic principles to create a self-sustaining ecosystem. It considers not only environmental factors but also cosmic and spiritual aspects of agriculture.

B Corp Certification: B Corp certification is given to companies that meet rigorous standards of social and environmental performance, accountability, and transparency. While not specific to food, many food companies hold this certification to demonstrate their commitment to sustainability and responsible business practices.

7. Party Plan Responsibly

Did you know that waste increases significantly during the holiday season? On average, it increases 25 percent between Thanksgiving and New Year's. A lot of that has to do with giving and receiving presents, but food waste also skyrockets, thanks to parties and events.

While I don't have stats on holiday parties, I do have stats on weddings. On average, a single wedding can waste 20 to 30 percent of its food. Wedding planners and caterers err on the side of caution to ensure there's enough food for everyone, which results in a lot of leftovers. Large spreads, elaborate food displays, and multiple food stations can also result in a lot of uneaten food.

If you're planning a large event with a caterer, tell them you want to prioritize efficient food management. Make sure you have RSVPs and consider donating excess food to local charities or food banks, or repurposing leftovers for post-wedding events or meals.

Here are a few more tips:

Plan the menu thoughtfully: Estimate the number of guests and plan your menu accordingly. Consider the portion sizes and avoid overordering or preparing excessive amounts of food. Opt for dishes that can be easily scaled up or down based on the number of attendees.

Send out RSVPs: Encourage your guests to RSVP so that you can have a more accurate count of attendees. Once you have this number, use a food calculator to figure out the recommended amount of food you'll need for each person.

Use small plates: My aunt hosts college kids every week for dinner. She puts out 10-inch plates instead of the average 12-inch plate to prevent excessive food waste, and then guests can always go back for more if they're still hungry.

Store and repurpose leftovers: If there are leftovers at the end of the party, store them properly and repurpose them for future meals. Leftover meats can be used in sandwiches or salads, vegetables can be added to soups or stir-fries, and bread can be turned into Croutons (page 185) or bread crumbs (see the Pro Tip on page 186).

Offer guests to-go containers: When I throw a dinner party, on the invitation, I ask guests to bring their own reusable containers for leftovers. I highly recommend this practice for all holiday meals, but especially Thanksgiving. I also keep a few containers on hand just in case someone forgot theirs.

Compost food scraps: Set up a designated compost bin for food scraps at the party. Educate your guests about composting and encourage them to dispose of their food waste properly (see Tip 11 on page 46).

8. Shop Seasonally

When I lived in California, my favorite Saturday activity was hitting up the local café for an iced coffee in my own cup before walking down to the farmers' market—the best bargain in town. That's where I bought the bulk of my groceries for the week.

Farmers' markets, which primarily sell local and seasonal produce, can offer competitive or lower prices compared to supermarkets. I could buy two artichokes for $2 at the farmers' market, but the exact same produce from the same farm was going for $4 at the grocery store. And according to the USDA, local and seasonal produce can often be more cost-effective due to reduced transportation costs and shorter supply chains. This can result in lower prices compared to imported or out-of-season foods.

A lot of the food in our grocery stores is imported. The next time you head to your local supermarket, check the country of origin and see just how far that produce had to travel. This concept is known as food miles and aims to highlight the environmental impact associated with the long-distance transportation of food. When you choose locally grown produce, the distance traveled from farm to plate is minimized, resulting in lower emissions from transportation. Food in the United States typically travels about 1,500 miles to reach consumers.

From a taste perspective, seasonal fruits and vegetables are generally more flavorful. If you've ever plucked something from a local garden at peak ripeness, you know just how fresh and delicious homegrown can be. So, if you enjoy gardening, that's the best way to reduce your food miles. I would personally love to garden (see Idealized Kathryn on page 8), but I am quite poor at it. The best I can do is try to shop in season, and have created a handy seasonal guide to fruits and vegetables for the northern hemisphere:

SPRING (MARCH, APRIL, MAY)

Fruits: Strawberries, rhubarb

Vegetables: Asparagus, spinach, peas, radishes, artichokes, spring onions

SUMMER (JUNE, JULY, AUGUST)

Fruits: Berries (strawberries, blueberries, raspberries, blackberries), cherries, peaches, apricots, watermelon, melons

Vegetables: Tomatoes, zucchini, corn, bell peppers, cucumbers, green beans, eggplant, lettuce, carrots, beets, summer squash

AUTUMN (SEPTEMBER, OCTOBER, NOVEMBER)

Fruits: Apples, pears, grapes, plums, persimmons, figs, cranberries, pomegranates

Vegetables: Pumpkins, winter squash, sweet potatoes, Brussels sprouts, cauliflower, broccoli, cabbage, kale, radicchio, mushrooms

WINTER
(DECEMBER, JANUARY, FEBRUARY)

Fruits: Citrus fruits (oranges, grapefruits, lemons, mandarins), pomegranates, kiwi

Vegetables: Winter greens (kale, collard greens, Swiss chard), cabbage, Brussels sprouts, broccoli, cauliflower, potatoes, turnips, rutabagas, onions, winter squash

9. Shop Locally

When it comes to seasonal and local produce, there are a few different places where I like to shop. While I still shop at large grocery stores, I also try to support local and smaller grocery markets, such as a produce stand, co-op, or farmers' market.

As discussed earlier, shopping locally results in fresher and tastier food. It has a lower carbon footprint, while also supporting your local economy. When you shop locally, you directly contribute to your community. Your purchases support local farmers, producers, and businesses, helping to create jobs and foster economic growth within your neighborhood. This circulation of money within the local economy can have an incredibly positive impact on the overall prosperity of your region.

Shopping locally also provides an opportunity to develop a deeper connection with your food and the people who produce it. You can meet local farmers, ask questions about their practices, and learn about the origins of the food you consume. This connection fosters a sense of community and a better understanding and appreciation of our food systems.

Another great way to connect with your local food systems is to go to a local farmers' market or join a CSA, which stands for Community Supported Agriculture. To become a member of a CSA, you sign up and pay a fee at the beginning of the growing season. This fee helps cover the costs of running the farm, such as buying seeds, paying for labor, and maintaining equipment.

Throughout the growing season, you'll receive regular deliveries or pick up your share of the farm's harvest. You'll get a variety of fresh vegetables, fruits, herbs, and sometimes even eggs or dairy, depending on the CSA you join and the local growing conditions. *(If you're going to be buying animal products, buying them locally from farms focused on regenerative agriculture practices is the most sustainable option after removal and reduction.)*

This type of program helps farmers by providing them with a stable market for their produce, and it gives you an opportunity to connect with the people who grow your food. Plus, you get to promote a more sustainable, resilient, and localized food system. Similarly, you might be interested in joining your local food co-op.

A food co-op is a type of cooperative business that focuses on providing its members with access to high-quality, sustainably sourced, and often locally produced food. It operates based on the principles of democratic control and shared ownership. In a food co-op, members come together to create a grocery store or market that meets their specific needs and aligns with their values.

What sets a food co-op apart from a traditional grocery store is the active participation of its members. In a food co-op, the customers are also the owners. Members pool their resources, both financially and through volunteer work, to establish and maintain the co-op. They have a say in the decision-making process, including selecting products, setting prices, and determining the overall direction of the store.

Joining a food co-op offers numerous benefits, such as providing a reliable source of fresh, local, and often organic food. Food co-ops prioritize sustainability and ethical practices, supporting local farmers and suppliers, as well as offering a wide selection of organic, natural, and environmentally friendly products. In my experience, co-ops have a large selection of bulk foods and are happy and well equipped for you to bring your own bags and jars to reduce food packaging. Plus, it's a great way to connect with like-minded individuals who value healthy and sustainable living.

10. Adopt a Plant-Rich Diet

Animal agriculture is a major contributor to greenhouse gas emissions. According to the Food and Agriculture Organization (FAO), the livestock sector accounts for approximately 14.5 percent of global greenhouse gas emissions.

The water footprint of meat and dairy production is also significantly higher compared to plant-based foods. For example, producing a pound of beef requires around 1,800 gallons of water, whereas producing a pound of vegetables typically requires less than 100 gallons.

Livestock farming requires vast amounts of land for grazing and feed production. This can lead to deforestation and habitat loss, endangering countless species. The World Wildlife Fund reports that approximately 80 percent of deforestation in the Amazon rainforest is linked to cattle ranching. Animal agriculture demands substantial resources, such as feed, land, water, and energy; and the production of plant-based foods is generally more resource-efficient.

According to a study published in the journal *Science*, plant-based diets have a significantly lower environmental footprint compared to diets rich in animal products. In addition, a study published in the journal Global Food Security estimates that approximately 36 percent of the world's crop calories are used as animal feed.[*]

---

[*] Emily S. Cassidy et al, "Redefining Agricultural Yields: From Tonnes to People Nourished per Hectacre," *Environmental Research Letters* 8, no. 3 (2013): 034015, https://doi.org/10.1088/1748-9326/8/3/034015.

We could feed significantly more people by adopting a more plant-based diet. I understand that transitioning to a vegan diet doesn't work for everyone, but I do believe that we all should be adding more plants to our plates. To get started, try swapping out one meal a day. For breakfast, make your oatmeal or chia seed pudding with soy milk or almond milk instead of cow's milk. If you're looking for something a bit more savory, try making a tofu breakfast scramble loaded up with your favorite veggies and spices.

The CDC reports that only about 1 in 10 Americans meet the daily recommended intake for fruits and vegetables, and we fall well below the recommended daily intake of fiber, but according to the FAO, Americans are now among the top per capita meat consumers in the world. The average American eats more than three times the global average, which in 2020 added up to about 264 pounds of meat per person, according to a study at the University of Illinois.

Adopting a more plant-rich diet that includes fruits, vegetables, and legumes will reduce your carbon footprint, conserve water, and should bump up increase essential nutrients, including fiber.

11. Learn to Compost

Composting is my number one tip for anyone who's looking to reduce their waste. It's estimated that 50 percent of an average household's waste can be cut with just this one simple swap. A lot of people think that their food scraps will break down in a landfill, which on the surface makes sense. After all, a landfill is just a giant hole in the ground—but landfills are designed for storage, not decomposition.

When organic waste, such as food scraps and yard trimmings, is dumped in landfills, it breaks down without any oxygen. This process creates methane, a superstrong greenhouse gas that's way more potent than carbon dioxide. What I mean by potent is that it traps a lot more heat in the atmosphere.

The Environmental Protection Agency (EPA) says that methane accounts for about 20 percent of all greenhouse gas emissions in the United States, and landfills are responsible for almost a fifth of that. But here's the cool part: the solution is really easy. We can compost our food scraps instead of tossing them in the landfill.

Composting is the natural process of recycling organic materials into nutrient-rich soil. It involves the decomposition of organic matter, such as kitchen scraps, yard waste, and other biodegradable materials, by microorganisms, bacteria, fungi, and other decomposers. It's an incredibly valuable resource. Gardeners and farmers mix compost into their soil to enhance its structure, moisture retention, and nutrient content, resulting in more productive and resilient plants.

To be perfectly honest with you, I am a terrible composter.

Which gives me an extreme advantage in this section. I have tried almost every type of composting and have failed so many times that I can give you almost foolproof advice. The MOST important thing you need to know is that composting is all about achieving the right balance between carbon-rich and nitrogen-rich materials. Both are crucial for creating a well-balanced compost pile that functions optimally.

When composting is done correctly, the pile should emit a pleasant, earthy smell. If you encounter such issues as pests or unpleasant odors, it's likely an indication that your compost pile is out of balance. To ensure an ideal balance, aim for approximately 70 percent carbon-rich materials and 30 percent nitrogen-rich materials. The carbon-rich materials provide structure, absorb moisture, and provide a source of energy for the microorganisms involved in the decomposition process. Nitrogen-rich materials contribute to the overall nutrient content of the compost providing a source of protein for the microorganisms and helping facilitate the breakdown of organic matter.

Maintaining the right balance between carbon and nitrogen will leave you with high-quality, nutrient-rich compost that will enhance the health and fertility of your soil.

CARBON-RICH MATERIALS (OFTEN REFERRED TO AS "BROWNS")

- Dry leaves
- Straw or hay
- Shredded newspaper
- Cardboard or paperboard (without glossy coatings—pizza boxes included)

- Wood chips or sawdust
- Corn stalks or dry corn husks
- Pine needles
- Twigs and branches (chopped or shredded)
- Dried plant materials (e.g., dried flowers or stalks)

NITROGEN-RICH MATERIALS (OFTEN REFERRED TO AS "GREENS")

- Fruit and vegetable scraps
- Coffee grounds and filters
- Tea leaves and tea bags (remove any staples)
- Grass clippings (free of herbicides and pesticides)
- Fresh plant trimmings (e.g., spent flowers, garden trimmings)
- Seaweed or kelp
- Manure from herbivorous animals (e.g., horse, cow, rabbit)
- Green plant materials (e.g., young weeds, green leaves)

It's important to note that depending on your type of compost setup, some materials should be avoided, such as meat, dairy products, oily foods, and pet waste. Some of these items can attract pests or introduce harmful bacteria. Additionally, be mindful of any materials that may have been treated with chemicals or herbicides, as they can impact the quality of the compost too.

Here are a few of the most common types of composting bins you can choose from:

THE BOKASHI METHOD

The *bokashi* method of composting is a unique and efficient way to convert organic waste into nutrient-rich compost. Originating in Japan, this utilizes a special mix of beneficial microorganisms to break down organic matter, including food scraps, into a fermented product called bokashi.

The process begins by layering food waste, such as fruit and vegetable scraps, meat, dairy, and even small amounts of cooked food, in an airtight container. The containers are usually about the size of an under-the-sink trash can, so it has a minimal footprint. Each layer is sprinkled with a bokashi inoculant, which consists of a combination of beneficial microbes, typically in the form of wheat bran or sawdust. These microorganisms, including lactic acid bacteria and yeast, ferment the organic waste instead of decomposing it through traditional aerobic composting.

Once the bokashi fermentation is complete, the material can be buried directly in the soil, so it can easily be mixed with traditional compost piles. Bokashi composting offers the advantage of being able to compost a wider range of food waste, including meat and dairy, which are typically discouraged in traditional composting methods.

It's a compact, convenient, and efficient way to compost organic waste, reducing its volume, preventing odors, and producing a valuable nutrient-rich product for your plants and gardens. I'd honestly recommend adding the bokashi bin if you have a stand-alone bin or a tumble bin.

TUMBLE BIN COMPOSTER

A tumble bin composter is particularly suitable for individuals or households with limited space. It's perfect if you have a small patio or a balcony in your home or apartment. It's one of the easiest and most efficient ways to produce high-quality compost in a shorter time. If your tumble bin gets direct sunlight, in warmer weather, you could go from scrap to soil in as little as two weeks.

The container is usually cylindrical and mounted on a frame making it easy to turn. You can buy them with one or two compartments. I recommend two compartments so you never have any downtime. Using the composter is simple. You add organic waste materials, such as kitchen scraps and yard waste, to the container, close the lid securely, and then rotate or tumble it regularly. This mixing action ensures proper aeration and enhances decomposition.

The benefits of using a tumble bin composter are numerous. It speeds up composting time by promoting a quicker breakdown of organic matter. Your food scraps can break down in as little as two weeks during the summer when the bin gets direct sunlight. The increased aeration prevents odors and encourages the growth of beneficial microorganisms, and the enclosed design helps contain heat, further accelerating decomposition and minimizing pest access.

VERMICOMPOSTING

Vermicomposting is a method of composting that utilizes worms, typically red wigglers, to break down your food scraps. They are highly efficient at consuming and decomposing organic matter, but quite temperamental. They are like pets and prefer to be indoors, unless you get one of the bins that can be buried in your garden. In vermicomposting, a container or bin is set up with bedding material, such as shredded newspaper or cardboard, along with the organic waste. The worms feed on the organic waste and break it down into nutrient-rich castings, worm poop, also known as vermicompost.

Vermicomposting offers several advantages. It can be done indoors or in small spaces, making it suitable for apartment dwellers or those with limited outdoor areas. However, it has a few more limitations because you'll really need to limit feeding the worms citrus, processed foods, onion, and garlic on top of avoiding the usual things like meat and dairy.

UPRIGHT COMPOST BIN

An upright compost bin, also known as a vertical compost bin or a standing compost bin, is a type of composting system that has an open bottom that's placed directly on the earth. There's a lid on top that you can remove to pour in your food scraps. To aerate the compost, you have to do it manually with a compost turner, shovel, or pitchfork.

Some models feature removable sections or doors for convenient harvesting of finished compost. I currently have one of these in my back garden that I don't use very frequently. It takes a long time for the food scraps to decompose in this style of bin, and it's not my favorite.

PICK-UP SERVICE

This is my absolute favorite type of composting because it's completely hands-off. The process usually involves regularly scheduled pickups, just like a normal trash day. The service provider will typically supply a bucket you can fill up and then will replace it with an empty bin when it's full.

Your food scraps are taken to a composting facility, where

they undergo the composting process to be transformed into nutrient-rich soil. Most services offered use a high-heat facility which means similar to the bokashi bin, you can compost anything. It's superconvenient and is becoming increasingly popular in urban areas, so check to see whether there's a local business or if your city is providing these services near you.

WHAT TO DO WITH YOUR COMPOST IF YOU DON'T HAVE A GARDEN?

Even if you don't have a garden, there are still several options for what you can do with your compost.

Donate it: You can donate your compost to community gardens, local farms, or neighbors who have gardens. Many gardening enthusiasts would gladly accept nutrient-rich compost to nourish their plants and soil. You can also offer it up for free on your local buy-nothing group or on Marketplace, etc.

Offer it to friends or family: If you have friends or family members with gardens, they might be interested in receiving your compost. You can offer it to them as a valuable resource to enhance their gardening efforts.

Share it with local gardening clubs or organizations: Look for local gardening clubs, urban farming initiatives, or environmental organizations in your area. They may have community projects or public spaces that could benefit from your compost donation.

Offer it to schools or other educational institutions: Schools, colleges, and other educational institutions with gardening programs often appreciate donations of compost. They can use it to teach students about sustainable gardening practices or to improve their campus landscaping.

Use it in potted plants or indoor gardening: Even without a garden, you can still utilize compost in potted plants or indoor gardening. Mix small amounts of compost into the potting soil to provide some added nutrients and improve your soil quality.

Remember, compost can benefit various gardening and landscaping projects, and I promise people will want it. So, don't let that hold you back from composting!

12. Garden and Regrow

Gardening is an incredibly sustainable form of food production. It creates a hyperlocalized system that can be resource-efficient and allows you to have total control over sustainable practices. It might be odd, but I always think about World War II when I think about local gardens.

During World War II, victory gardens played a significant role in supplementing the food supply and promoting self-sufficiency. According to the National WWII Museum, victory gardens were estimated to have produced about 40 percent of the fresh vegetables consumed in the United States. This contribution helped alleviate pressure on the commercial food system, which was redirecting resources toward the war effort.

Victory gardens were encouraged and promoted through government campaigns, and millions of Americans participated in growing their own food.

I often wonder how our food system would change if we all had small gardens that at least supplemented some of our groceries. There's been a resurgence of gardening and local food production in recent years thanks to the rise of urban agriculture, community gardens, and the farm-to-table movement.

The National Gardening Association estimates that, in 2020, over 18 million households in the United States participated in food gardening, collectively producing billions of dollars' worth of fresh produce. However, the scale has still not reached the level of victory gardens during WWII.

According to the EPA, the average lawn size in the United States is around 0.2 acres, collectively covering about 40 million acres—larger than the state of Georgia. The water required to sustain all this grass can account for approximately 50 to 75 percent of a household's water usage. Making grass—yes, grass—the largest irrigated agricultural "crop" in the United States, surpassing corn, wheat, and fruit orchards *combined*.

If all these lawns, or even part of these lawns were converted into productive gardens, it could potentially yield a substantial amount of food producing a diverse range of fruits, vegetables, and herbs throughout the growing season. While we wouldn't be able to meet the entire food demand of the country, we'd be in a much better position.

It is worth noting that the context and motivations for gardening have changed over time. Victory gardens were a response to a specific wartime need, whereas today, home gardening often reflects a desire for sustainable living, access to fresh and organic produce, and a connection to nature.

I don't have a lot of outside space, but one of my big goals over the next few years is to set up a container garden on my back deck. If you're also limited in outdoor space, you could consider joining a community garden, which is a shared space where individuals or groups come together to grow plants, vegetables, herbs, and flowers collectively. It's typically a piece of land that's divided into smaller plots or shared spaces where community members can cultivate their own plants. These gardens can serve as a hub for community engagement, education, and social interaction. Plus, they usually offer composting, which is one of the best eco-friendly swaps you can make.

CHAPTER 2

MAXIMIZING YOUR PRODUCE

After returning from the grocery store, it's time to store and prep the food you bought. Set yourself up for success by setting aside 30 minutes to prep your food. Store your produce to maximize its life expectancy and get a head start on chopping. Prechopped vegetables can significantly expedite meal preparation during the week. You're way more likely to eat the food you bought (*i.e., prevent it from going to waste*) if you can get homemade meals on the table quickly.

If you don't have enough time to start chopping when you get home from the grocery store, try thinking in terms of several fairly immediate uses. For example, if a recipe for today requires half an onion for a stir-fry, chop the entire onion and save the unused portion for tomorrow's dish—this time-saving technique allows you to chop once and eat twice.

If you only take one thing away from this chapter, the next three tips here are what I want you to follow. If I'm busy after unloading my groceries, these are the only three tips I adhere to, and I've still seen great results. Throughout this chapter, though, we'll get more into the nitty-gritty of produce storage and work out how exactly to maximize all of your produce!

13. Wait, Don't Wash

When storing your produce, you might be tempted to wash it all, first thing, when you get home. A lot of internet tips suggest prewashing produce with baking soda or vinegar when you get home from the store, and I strongly advise against it, especially for delicate berries.

Washing fruits and vegetables introduces moisture, which can accelerate spoilage. It's best to wash them just before consumption to maintain their freshness (see Tip 19 on page 70 when you're ready to wash).

14. Protect Your Greens

When storing greens, such as lettuce or spinach, it's helpful to place them in an airtight container along with a cloth napkin. The napkin will absorb any excess moisture, preventing the greens from becoming soggy and wilted. If you buy your greens in a plastic clamshell, the next time you open the clamshell to get some, add the napkin. If you buy your greens in a plastic bag, get them out of there and place them in an airtight container, such as a reusable, lidded bin or a mason jar.

15. Prioritize, Prioritize, Prioritize

Prioritize consuming food that is prone to spoilage sooner rather than later. For instance, eat your butter lettuce first and save kale for the end of the week. Prioritize your berries over your apples, and so on. By doing so, you can reduce food waste and ensure that these items are enjoyed at their peak freshness.

> **Pro Tip:** *If you still struggle to eat all of your produce before it goes bad, make an eat-me-first box. Before you put your new produce away, gather the leftover produce from the week before in an organizational bin so you can easily see what needs to be eaten first.*

16. Know Your Fridge Zones

A quick way to save money on your power bill and reduce food waste is to make sure that your fridge is set to the right temperature. This will ensure food safety and prevent the growth of harmful bacteria. The optimal energy-saving temperature for refrigerators is typically between 35° and 38°F and the freezer section should be set to 0°F.

It's also important to note that different areas in the fridge fluctuate in temperature. For instance, the upper shelves are colder than the shelves in the door. It's not only about how you store your produce, but where you store it, too. Organization plays into this as well because you want your fridge full, but not overcrowded so air can flow for proper circulation and cooling. Avoid blocking the air vents inside of your fridge because that can lead to uneven temperature distribution.

Upper Shelves: The upper shelves of a refrigerator are consistently cool, but a little warmer than other areas. This is a great place to store leftovers, ready-to-eat foods, and drinks. This should also put these foods at eye level to encourage you to eat those leftovers first so they don't go to waste.

Lower Shelves: The lower shelves of the fridge maintain the coldest temperatures. They're ideal for storing dairy, eggs, and raw meats. It's best to keep raw meat separate from other foods to avoid cross-contamination, and keep it on a plate or a tray to prevent any drips or spills onto other food items.

Crisper Drawers: Crisper drawers create a more humid environment perfect for storing fruits and vegetables. These drawers help retain moisture and prevent produce from drying out or wilting quickly. Take note of which produce items produce ethylene and try to keep them separate, as they will cause some produce to ripen more quickly

Door Shelves: The refrigerator door is the most prone to temperature fluctuations because it's consistently being opened and closed. It's the best place to store condiments, sauces, dressings, and other items that have higher acidity or preservatives, since these products are typically more resistant to temperature changes.

Pro Tip: *Did you know refrigerators account for approximately 8 to 15 percent of a household's total energy usage? They're one of the most significant contributors to the power bill outside of heating and cooling. To maintain optimal energy efficiency and prolong the lifespan of your refrigerator, it's crucial to clean the coils regularly. Over time, dust and debris can accumulate on the coils at the back or bottom of the fridge. If you have a pet, and especially if you have a husky like me, all of that hair hinders the cooling efficiency. Regularly vacuuming your coils will keep your fridge running efficiently, reduce your energy consumption, and help your fridge maintain proper temperature levels.*

Freezer: Utilize your freezer to store frozen fruits, vegetables, meats, precooked meals, ice cream, and other frozen items. Proper packaging, such as airtight containers or freezer bags, can help maintain the quality of the food and prevent freezer burn. With the freezer, you can extend the shelf life of various ingredients. See Tip 20 on page 71 for more information.

17. Store Your Produce Right

Here are a few simple ways I store my produce to extend its life. By adopting a few of these practices, plus sticking to a list and following one of the meal plans, you'll be able to eat everything relatively quickly. I don't pay too much attention to ethylene, but I think it's worth noting if you're buying a lot of produce at one time.

STORE IN A COOL, DARK, DRY SPOT

Bananas: Disassemble the bunch and store as single bananas. Store in a bowl by themselves if you have the space.

Garlic and onions: Store in a dark cabinet, and keep them away from potatoes.

Potatoes and sweet potatoes: Store in a dark cabinet, and keep them away from onions and shallots.

RIPEN AT ROOM TEMPERATURE, THEN MOVE TO THE FRIDGE

This type of produce doesn't need to be stored any special way. It can sit on a shelf or in the crisper drawer.

Apricots

Avocados

Guavas

Kiwifruit

Mangoes

Melons

Nectarines

Papayas

Passion fruit

Peaches

Pears

Persimmons

Pineapples

Plantains

Plums

Tomatoes

KEEP IN THE REFRIGERATOR

Artichokes: Spritz with water and store in a bowl.

Asparagus: Place the stalks in a cup of water like a bouquet of flowers.

Beets: Remove the greens, chop, and place in an airtight container, such as a mason jar. Use the greens like spinach and wash right before using. Store the beets loose and whole.

Broccoli: Cut off and discard the very end of the stalks and place the stalks upright in a jar of water like a bouquet of flowers.

Brussels sprouts: Store in an airtight mason jar.

Cabbage: Store loose in the crisper drawer after it's cut, store like romaine and spinach.

Carrots: Store submerged in a glass of water. Swap out the water every 2 to 3 days.

Cauliflower: Store loose in the crisper drawer

Celery: Store submerged in a glass of water. Swap out the water every 2 to 3 days.

Cherries: Store in an airtight mason jar.

Corn: Store loose in the crisper drawer with the husk on.

Cranberries: Store in an airtight mason jar.

Cucumbers: Store in an upright silicone bag or an airtight container with a cloth towel inside.

Eggplants: Store loose in the crisper drawer

Figs: Wrap in a tea towel.

Grapes: Store in a bowl on a shelf.

Green beans: Store in a silicone bag or an airtight container

Green onions: Store, root down, in a cup of water.

Kale: Chop and place in an airtight container, such as a mason jar or large mixing bowl with a lid. Wash right before eating.

Leeks: Store loose in the crisper drawer.

Lettuce: Chop and place in an airtight container, such as a mason jar or large mixing bowl with a lid, with a thin cloth napkin on top. Wash right before eating.

Mushrooms: Store open in a bowl on a shelf or in a brown paper bag.

Peas: Store in an airtight mason jar,

Radishes: Remove the greens, chop, and place in an airtight container, such as a mason jar. Use the greens with other salad greens and wash right before using. Store the radishes loose.

Rhubarb: Wrap in a tea towel.

Spinach: Chop and place in an airtight container, such as a mason jar or large mixing bowl with a lid, and add a thin cloth napkin on top. Wash right before eating.

Turnips: Chop and keep in an airtight mason jar,

Zucchini: Store loose in the crisper drawer.

18. Watch Out for Ethylene

Certain fruits and veggies release a natural plant hormone called ethylene. This can speed up the ripening process for nearby produce. To prevent overripening or premature spoilage, consider storing ethylene-releasing produce and ethylene-sensitive items separately.

ETHYLENE-PRODUCING FRUITS

Apples
Avocados
Bananas
Kiwis
Mangoes

Melons (e.g., cantaloupe, honeydew, and watermelon)
Peaches
Pears
Plums

ETHYLENE-SENSITIVE FRUITS

Berries (strawberries, raspberries, blueberries)
Citrus fruits (oranges, lemons, limes, grapefruits)

Grapes
Pineapples

ETHYLENE-PRODUCING VEGETABLES

Asparagus

Broccoli

Brussels sprouts

Cabbage

Carrots

Green beans

Peas

Tomatoes

ETHYLENE-SENSITIVE VEGETABLES

Leafy greens (lettuce,
    spinach, kale)

Cucumbers

Peppers

Potatoes

Squash (zucchini,
    yellow squash,
    butternut squash)

19. Wash Before Use

I typically just wash my produce in water and I do it right before I'm getting ready to cook or eat it. But if you need something a little more heavy-duty, try using a mixture of water and vinegar. If you want to make your own vinegar, see Tip 24 on page 84.

1. Fill a large bowl with water.
2. Add 1 part white vinegar to 4 parts water. This ratio can vary, but a common guideline is ¼ cup of vinegar for every cup of water.
3. Place the fruits and vegetables into the water-vinegar mixture and let them soak for 5 to 10 minutes.
4. Gently scrub the produce with your hands or a vegetable brush to remove any dirt, debris, or residues.
5. Rinse the fruits and vegetables thoroughly under running water to remove the vinegar solution.

Vinegar can help remove dirt, bacteria, and pesticide residues from the surface of your produce. It has disinfectant properties and can help break down waxy coatings on certain fruits and vegetables.

20. Utilize Your Freezer

Your freezer is a food waste–fighting workhorse. If utilized properly, you can easily save food before it goes bad and extend its life. If your peppers or mushrooms are starting to wrinkle, you can easily cut them up and freeze them for later. Almost anything can be frozen, including meat, fish, fruits, bread, vegetables, and even liquids. Freezing fresh produce is an excellent method to preserve its quality and prevent spoilage.

I also like to use my freezer to enjoy produce beyond its seasonal availability without the need for canning. It's a great way to shop in season, buy fruits and vegetables when they're at their cheapest, and be able to enjoy them all year round. You can bet I'll have a few bags of blueberries from the u-pick farm I visit this year.

Here are some tips for freezing different types of food:

Bread: Bread freezes so well. Whether that's tortillas, bagels, baguettes, whole loaves, or even your sandwich bread. It's best to put the bread in presliced so you can grab what you need for sandwiches. The bread will stay as fresh as the day you bought it. I've stored my bread in an old pillowcase—clean, obviously, as well as an old paper bag. It should last for about 2 months.

Fruit: Freezing fruit is simple and great for making smoothies or desserts like ice cream. Spread the fruit out on a baking sheet and freeze until solid, then transfer it to a glass, metal container, or reusable silicone bag. Keep in mind that frozen fruit has a high water content. Once defrosted, it won't maintain its original integrity. It's best used for things like baking, compote, jam, or smoothies.

Tomatoes: Tomatoes don't freeze well on their own, due to their high water content. If you notice your tomatoes starting to go bad or if you have a bumper crop, use them to make sauces or spreads. Try making tomato sauce or salsa (see Tip 45 on page 121) and pouring it into clean, old pasta sauce jars before freezing. There's no need to buy new jars just for freezer storage. Just make sure you don't fill the jars too full. (See Tip 21 on page 74 for full instructions.)

Beans: Cooking dried beans in a slow cooker is a cost-effective and convenient way to have ready-to-eat beans. A 1-pound bag of dried beans at my local grocery store costs $1.45. A pound of dried beans will make about 4½ cans' worth of beans. You can cook your beans in a slow cooker overnight and then freeze the leftovers in mason jars or reusable silicone jars. If you need to defrost them quickly, just place them in a bowl of water for about 30 minutes.

Veggies: If you have a lot of veggies from your garden or just a few about to go bad, wash, dry, and cut the vegetables into how you would normally use them in a recipe. Place them on a baking sheet, freeze until solid, and then transfer them to a lidded container and place back in the freezer. You can easily grab just what you need for a recipe.

Liquids: When freezing liquids, such as soups, sauces, or broths, leave some headspace in the container to accommodate expansion. Liquids expand when frozen, so this will prevent your containers from cracking or bursting. It's also advisable to cool the liquids in the refrigerator, before transferring them to the freezer, reducing the risk of temperature shock. As a note, you also shouldn't put hot foods directly into the fridge as it will lower the temperature of everything else in there. Allow piping hot foods to cool for a bit before storing.

Pro Tip: *Plan a freezer night! I mostly store two things in my freezer: fruit for smoothies, and tortillas. Every year for my birthday and Christmas, my dad sends me about 100 tortillas from my favorite spot in San Antonio. They're the best tortillas in the world. (See Tip 74 on page 183 for more on freezing bread.) Everything else in my freezer goes there to die, and I don't want that to happen to you. Don't let your freezer be a layover spot between the fridge and compost bin. Every two weeks, plan a freezer night. You can even add this night to your meal plan in case you need additional ingredients to make a full meal. Now you can actually eat the food that you've frozen, and clear up valuable freezer space for the important things . . . like a year's supply of the world's best tortillas.*

21. Practice Good Freezer Technique

To optimize your freezer and frozen foods, you should also try to perfect the following techniques:

Cooling: Cooked foods should be thoroughly cooled before placing them in the freezer. Properly cooling cooked foods at room temperature or in the refrigerator preserves their quality, inhibits the growth of harmful bacteria, and if you're using a glass container in the fridge, will prevent it from breaking.

Packaging: To preserve the flavor and texture of your food and prevent freezer burn, I use airtight containers like old lidded storage bins, mason jars (see next tip), and reusable silicone bags. These options provide a protective barrier against air and moisture.

Portioning: Before freezing, divide larger items, such as meat or vegetables, into smaller portions. By doing so, you can thaw only what you need for a particular meal, minimizing waste and ensuring the rest remains frozen for future use.

Labeling: If you have a large freezer, or you easily lose track of what/when you froze, make a label with the contents and the date they were frozen. You can easily identify and track the foods in your freezer, ensuring nothing is forgotten. I like to use washi tape, which is compostable.

Thawing: When it comes to thawing frozen items, avoid room-temperature thawing. Opt for safe thawing methods, such as defrosting in the refrigerator for approximately 24 hours. Alternatively, you can place the item in a bowl of cold water, changing the water every 30 minutes, or use the defrost option on a microwave, following the manufacturer's guidelines.

22. How to Freeze in Mason Jars

A lot of people think you can't freeze glass, but you absolutely can. It's a perfect way to upcycle old jam jars and pasta jars. See Tip 90 on page 207 for how to easily remove labels. Here are a few tips for the best practices, but the most important thing to remember is: don't overfill them.

There are two types of mason jars. There are jars with shoulders and jars without shoulders. You can freeze in both types of jars, but you shouldn't overfill them.

When filling the jars, leave enough headspace at the top to allow for expansion as the contents freeze. If you have a jar with straight sides leave 2 to 3 inches of space between the liquid and the lid. If you have a jar with shoulders, you want to leave 2 to 3 inches before the shoulder starts. This prevents the jars from cracking due to pressure buildup.

Let the food or liquid cool before pouring it into the jars. Hot or warm items can cause the jars to break when placed in the freezer. Let the contents cool to room temperature or refrigerate them before transferring them to the jars and to your freezer.

If you're still worried about your glass breaking, don't screw the lid on tight until after everything has frozen. Once frozen, tighten the lid. You can also buy lids specifically for freezing.

Use washi tape and a marker to write the contents and date on the jars so you can easily identify what's in each jar and use the oldest items first.

Place your jars in a sturdy position to prevent them falling over and getting damaged.

When you're ready to use the frozen food, transfer the jar from the freezer to the refrigerator and let it thaw slowly. For faster thawing, you can place the sealed jar in a bowl of cold water, changing the water every 30 minutes until the contents are fully thawed. (PS: Save that water to water your plants or garden!)

CHAPTER 3

SAVING YOUR FRUIT

The best way to reduce food waste is by planning ahead, shopping smarter, and storing food properly. During the first part of this book, we've focused primarily on all the ways you can actively minimize waste on the front end.

However, despite our best efforts in prepping and planning, things happen.

Maybe your garden produced a bumper crop, and you have more tomatoes than you could possibly use. Maybe a vacation kept you away a bit longer than you expected, and your citrus is starting to shrivel. Perhaps you found an amazing deal on avocados from the discounted section because they need to eaten ASAP (and, if you find yourself in this situation, you can pop whole avocados into the freezer and defrost them on the counter when you need to use them in a spread or dip).

In this section, we will delve into food-waste-fighting recipes, and this chapter is all about fruit. Just because your apple has lost its crisp or your banana is a bit too spotted doesn't mean you can't transform these less-than-peak fruits into delightful recipes.

The key is to work with the condition of your produce rather than against it. While a bruised apple may not taste the best when eaten raw, you can easily turn it into applesauce. Use the super-sweet, brown-spotted banana for banana bread. Mash or puree slightly mushy strawberries to transform them into a delectable jam or spread. These techniques allow you to embrace the full potential of your produce and create mouthwatering dishes.

APPLES

A is for apple. Just kidding—I promise I won't do that for the whole book. When I lived in Berkeley, there was an apple tree in our backyard, so we had *a lot* of apples. In the fall, I did a whole apple week on my blog. I made and tried all sorts of delicious apple recipes to *try* to make a dent in our very prolific tree. I made apple salad, apple cobbler, apple syrup for cocktails, apple sauce, apple scrap vinegar (very similar to apple cider vinegar ACV), and even filled a giant cardboard box with free fruit for our neighborhood.

Last year, after moving to Portland, Maine, I spent my first fall in New England. So, obviously, I had to go apple picking. I went with a group of friends and we all split a bushel. Thankfully, I already had an arsenal of recipes ready to go for making the most of this big harvest. Of all my recipe trialing in California, applesauce was clearly a fan favorite. Plus, it freezes really well!

23. Slow Cooker Applesauce

The best thing about this recipe is that it's really hard to mess up. Most of the recipes in this book are a bit rustic. For instance, I don't know how sweet your apples are. So, if you taste the recipe as you go, you can figure out whether you want a little more salt, acid, or sweetness to balance out the fruit you actually have.

MAKES APPROXIMATELY 4 CUPS

6 to 8 apples (save the peels and cores to make homemade vinegar, as in Tip 24 on page 84)

Juice of 1 lemon

Splash of pure vanilla extract

Pinch of ground cinnamon

Pinch of salt

Pure maple syrup (optional)

1. Peel and dice the apples. Set aside the peels and cores to use for making homemade vinegar (recipe follows). Place the peeled and diced apples in a slow cooker. Squeeze the lemon juice over the apples.

2. Add the vanilla, cinnamon, and salt to balance the sweetness and bring out the natural flavors of the apples. If desired, drizzle a small amount of maple syrup over the apples to enhance the sweetness. However, taste the apples first, as they may already be sweet enough on their own. Stir all the ingredients together until well combined.

3. Cover the slow cooker and cook on LOW for approximately 6 hours. The exact cooking time may vary depending on the type and ripeness of the apples, so check for your desired consistency.

4. After 6 hours, the apples should be soft and cooked down. You can use a potato masher or a fork to mash the apples to your preferred texture. If you prefer a smoother applesauce, use an immersion blender or transfer the mixture to a regular blender and blend until smooth.

5. Taste the applesauce and adjust the sweetness or seasoning, if needed. You can add more cinnamon, lemon juice, or maple syrup according to your preference. Once the applesauce reaches your desired consistency and flavor, transfer it to clean jars or containers, seal them, and store them in the refrigerator for up to a week.

NOTE: *If you only have one or two apples, you can easily scale this recipe down and do it on the stovetop. Or grate your mushy apple into oatmeal for a delicious breakfast!*

24. Homemade Apple Scrap Vinegar

Homemade vinegar has become my absolute favorite thing to make. I've made lemon peel vinegar, orange peel vinegar, pine needle vinegar using a branch from my Christmas tree, red wine vinegar, white wine vinegar, Champagne vinegar, and of course, the classic apple scrap vinegar. I'm not going to bore you with all those recipes, because once you make one vinegar, you've kind of made them all.

Homemade, infused vinegars have very similar mechanics, but they all start with this as the base. I typically use my homemade vinegars for both cleaning and cooking; I am partial to Strawberry Top Vinegar (page 104) and Leftover Red Wine Vinegar (page 227) for cooking.

MAKES APPROXIMATELY 3 CUPS

INGREDIENTS	EQUIPMENT
2 to 3 tablespoons sugar	A *very clean* glass jar
3 or 4 apple cores and peels	A swatch of cloth
Lukewarm filtered water	Some rubber bands

1. Thoroughly clean a glass jar to ensure it is free of any contaminants.
2. Place the sugar in the jar, followed by the apple cores and peels. Make sure all the apple remnants are fully submerged in the jar. Fill the jar with lukewarm filtered water, ensuring that the apples are completely submerged.

3. Take a clean swatch of cloth and, using rubber bands, securely fasten it over the mouth of the jar. This allows the liquid to breathe while keeping out any dust or insects.

4. Find a suitable location for the jar in a dark, dry, and cool cabinet. It's important to store it away from direct sunlight. Let the jar sit in the cabinet for 3 weeks. During this time, check periodically to ensure that the apple remnants remain submerged in the water. You may also notice bubbling and fermentation activity, which is a sign that the vinegar is developing.

5. After 3 weeks, filter out the apple remnants from the jar, using a fine-mesh strainer or cheesecloth. Compost the apple remnants. Return the strained liquid to the jar and cover it with the swatch of cloth (it can be the same one as long as it's still clean), then place it back in the cabinet for

an additional month. This allows the vinegar to mature and develop a stronger flavor.

6. Once the month is over, your homemade apple cider vinegar should be ready. It will have a distinct tangy aroma and flavor. Transfer to a clean glass bottle or jar with a solid lid, for storage. It can be kept at room temperature.

NOTE: *The vinegar should NOT grow mold; if it has grown mold, the batch has gone bad. This can happen because a piece of apple wasn't fully submerged in the liquid. You can watch for mold and also check the smell of your vinegar to make sure the batch stays fresh (do not taste it). During the first few weeks, the liquid should smell bright and pleasant. It should never smell rotten.*

25. Apple Peel Simmer Pot

Still have leftover apple scraps? Use them to make a simmer pot. This is an all-natural air freshener that will make your home smell divine. You can use all sorts of common food scraps, such as apple peels and cores, orange peels, herb ends and stems, and so on.

MAKES 1 POT

1 apple

1 bay leaf

2 cinnamon sticks

1½ teaspoons whole cloves

1 teaspoon pure vanilla extract

1 whole nutmeg

ON THE STOVETOP

1. Fill a small saucepan with water and bring to a boil. Then, add all your simmer pot ingredients and continue to boil for a few minutes.
2. Lower the heat to a simmer and add water as needed, usually every 30 minutes or so.

IN A SLOW-COOKER

1. Fill the slow cooker most of the way with water, add your ingredients, put on the lid, and set the slow cooker to HIGH.
2. When steam is rolling off the lid, remove the lid and set the slow cooker to LOW. Add water as needed to keep the simmer pot at least halfway full while using.

NOTE: *These simmer pots can be used for two to three hours or longer, provided that they're checked and monitored consistently.*

AVOCADOS

Avocados might not be the most frequently used produce, but they get a whole section in this book because they're incredibly temperamental.

26. Pick the Right Avocado

The best way to avoid wasting avocados is to pick the perfect one at the grocery store. I like to do a quick scan based on color and touch. Ripe avocados usually have a dark green or black skin color and yield slightly to gentle pressure when squeezed. Avoid avocados that are too soft or mushy unless you're going to eat them the same day.

I like to examine the stem end of the avocado. If the stem is resistant, it's not ripe yet. If the stem easily comes off and reveals green flesh underneath, it's likely ripe and ready to eat. However, if you find brown or black discoloration, the avocado may be overripe.

As with bananas, you might want to stagger the ripeness level of your avocados. Once it's at peak ripeness, you can prolong its state for two to three days in the fridge.

If your avocado isn't ripe enough, try placing it in a paper bag with a banana, to speed up the ripening process.

Pro Tip: *Avocados turn brown due to a process called oxidation. When the flesh of an avocado comes into contact with air, enzymes in the fruit react with oxygen, causing it to brown similar to apples. It's still safe to eat when it turns brown, but you can also cut away the brown or bruised parts. Of course, always use your best judgment; if the avocado is severely damaged or black, you'll probably want to consider composting it.*

27. Storing Half an Avocado

It's best to eat the avocado within 1 to 2 days, and if you keep running into problems, it might be worth trying a beeswax wrap or a Food Hugger® container designed to hug your avocado perfectly. I rarely eat a whole avocado in one sitting, and these are my top three methods for storing a half-eaten avocado, in order of efficacy.

The hat method: When storing your avocado, keep the pit intact. The pit helps slow down the oxidation process and prevents browning. Sprinkle a bit of lemon juice on the avocado flesh, place the removed peel from the other avocado half on top, and store it in the fridge.

The plate method: Remove the pit from the avocado half. Sprinkle the flesh with lemon juice, place face down on a plate, and store in the fridge.

In a container: Leave the pit in the avocado and sprinkle the flesh with a bit of lemon juice. Store in an airtight container with a chunk of red onion.

28. Save Your Avocado for Creating a Natural Dye

If you have an old, stained white T-shirt lying around, consider dyeing it with your leftover avocado peels and pits. It's a food waste–fighting and eco-friendly way to get a lovely shade of peach or pink.

1. You'll need at least three avocado pits and peels; you can store these in the freezer. The more pits you have, the stronger the dye will be. Before you freeze them, give them a good rinse to remove any residue of flesh.

2. If using fresh avocado pits and peels, remove any flesh remaining on them and give them a good rinse to clean off any residue.

3. Place the avocado pits in a large pot—large enough to later be able to immerse the fabric you wish to dye—and add enough water to cover them. Bring the water to a boil and then lower the heat to a simmer. Let the pits simmer for about an hour, or until the water turns a rich, reddish color.

4. Remove the avocado pits from the pot and strain the liquid to remove any remaining solids. You can use a fine-mesh strainer or cheesecloth for this.

5. Wet the T-shirt or fabric you wish to dye and soak it in a mixture of water and a mordant, such as alum or distilled white vinegar. This helps the fabric absorb and retain the dye.

6. Place the pretreated fabric in the pot of avocado dye and bring to a simmer. Let the fabric simmer for at least an hour, or until you achieve the desired color. Keep in mind that the color may appear lighter when the fabric is wet.

7. Remove the fabric from the dye bath and rinse it thoroughly with cool water until the water runs clear. Hang the fabric to air dry away from direct sunlight.

Remember, the intensity of the color may vary depending on such factors as the quantity of avocado pits used, the type of fabric, and the duration of dyeing. It's also worth experimenting with different fabric types and dyeing techniques to achieve unique and varied results. Enjoy your natural and sustainable avocado pit–dyed fabric!

BANANAS AND BANANA PEELS

Bananas are the most popular fruit in the United States, so I definitely feel I'm in the minority when I tell you that they're not my favorite. I'm not crazy about *banana flavor*. I prefer greener bananas, before they get that real strong, sweet banana taste, and I typically use them in smoothies because they are wonderful for muscle recovery. A greener banana is going to be less sweet, and starchier. A yellow banana with a few spots is going to be really sweet because those starches have broken down into sugar.

While the most popular, bananas are also the most thrown-away supermarket item. A study from Karlstad University in Sweden discovered that most bananas weren't bought if they had any brown spots, meaning perfectly fine bananas wound up in a dumpster. Grocers also tend to throw single bananas away at the end of the day. These are bananas that have been ripped off from their bunch. So, when you're shopping for bananas, pick single ones, and go for any that look perfectly ripe because they freeze incredibly well.

29. Freeze Your Bananas

If you struggle to eat all the bananas in your bunch, they freeze incredibly well and will last much longer this way! I make a lot of smoothies, and break my bananas in half and store them in a Stasher® bag in the freezer for 3 to 6 months. Then, I can pop them out and use them as needed. Afterward, you'll be left with quite a few peels (see Tip 30 on page 95).

30. Use Your Banana Peels

Although banana peels aren't commonly eaten in the United States, they're very popular in other countries and completely edible. Here are a few examples of common recipes that incorporate banana peels:

Banana Peel Curry: In India, banana peels are used in curries. The peels are typically cooked until tender and then added to a flavorful curry sauce with spices, herbs, and vegetables.

Banana Peel Stir-Fry: Banana peels can be sliced thinly and stir-fried with vegetables and seasonings. They can add a unique texture and flavor to the dish, similar to typically stir-fried vegetables.

Pulled Banana Peel BBQ: This was a viral food trend where banana peels were shredded into thin strips to mimic the texture of pulled pork. These were sautéed with barbecue sauce and served in a bun or on top of a potato.

Banana Peel Chutney: Banana peels are cooked down with spices, onions, and other ingredients to make a tangy and savory chutney. This chutney can be enjoyed as a condiment or dip with bread, crackers, or as an accompaniment to rice dishes.

NOTE: *When using banana peels in recipes, it's important to thoroughly wash and remove any labels, wax, or residue from the peels. Additionally, choosing organic bananas is recommended, to minimize exposure to pesticides or other chemicals.*

31. (Overripe) Banana Bread

As we all know, bananas can go from your perfect level of sweetness to wayyyy too mushy and sweet in a matter of 24 hours. So, what do you do with those mushy bananas? Make banana bread! I know I said I wasn't crazy about banana flavor, but this is my exception to the rule. I love a good thick piece of banana bread that's been toasted on each side and smothered in peanut butter. This is one of my husband's favorite recipes, and I swear he used to hide bunches of bananas in cabinets so they'd appear past their prime and I'd have to make banana bread because I didn't want them to go to waste.

MAKES 1 LOAF

Olive oil for the pan
1¾ cups all-purpose flour
¼ cup sugar
1 teaspoon baking powder
1 teaspoon baking soda

Pinch of salt
3 large overripe bananas
⅓ cup olive oil
¼ cup almond milk
1 teaspoon pure vanilla extract

1. Preheat your oven to 350°F and spray a 9-by-4-inch loaf pan with olive oil (I use a Misto). It's reusable, and you can pour oil into it and turn it into a spray.
2. Combine the flour, sugar, baking powder, baking soda, and salt in a small bowl and stir well.
3. In a large bowl, mash the bananas until mostly smooth (I like as few lumps as possible). Then, add the olive oil, almond milk, and vanilla to the mashed banana and stir to incorporate.

4. Add the flour mixture to the banana mixture and stir again to combine, but be careful not to overmix.

5. Transfer the batter to your prepared loaf pan and sprinkle on any toppings. Bake for 1 hour, or until a toothpick comes out clean, and remove from the oven. Allow to cool and then enjoy plain or toasted!

NOTE: *If you'd like, you can jazz up the banana bread batter with some vegan chocolate chips, walnuts, or whatever your heart desires.*

BERRIES

While growing up, I didn't eat a lot of fruit. I'm not sure why, but my family didn't really buy or eat it. I still remember the first time I had a blueberry. It was Tech Sunday for a production of *Hair* I was in, and my friend had a container full of the most beautiful strawberries and blueberries. It was July, the absolute peak season, and she was kind enough to share. Blueberries have been my favorite fruit ever since. So much so that one of my dear friends made me a Maine blueberry pie for Christmas. I'm eagerly counting down the days until I can go blueberry picking this summer, and if I'm lucky, I can talk him into sharing that pie recipe. I'm going to freeze a bunch of them and make smoothies, muffins, and, hopefully, pie.

Berries can go bad quickly, so it's best to store them properly. I recommend airtight mason jars, in which they can stay good for up to 2 weeks. The tight seal formed by the jar's lid blocks out oxygen, moisture, and other potential factors that contribute to spoilage and deterioration. But if your berries start to get mushy, you can still turn them into some of the most delicious recipes! Mushy berries are perfect for fruit leather, compote, jam, and more.

32. Blueberry Compote

If your berries have started to turn to mush, you can play into their texture by creating a compote. I love nothing more than spooning heaps of compote onto pancakes fresh off the griddle. But, of course, you can also use it for yogurt, ice cream, oatmeal, waffles, and other desserts. This compote will stay good in your fridge for about a week.

MAKES APPROXIMATELY ½ CUP

1 cup fresh blueberries

1 tablespoon pure maple syrup

1 tablespoon water

1 tablespoon fresh lemon juice

½ teaspoon pure
    vanilla extract

1. Combine ¾ cup of the blueberries with the maple syrup, water, lemon juice, and vanilla in a small saucepan. Simmer over medium heat, stirring occasionally, for about 10 minutes. This will help break down the blueberries and create a flavorful base.
2. After 10 minutes, add the remaining ¼ cup of blueberries to the saucepan. Continue to cook, stirring occasionally, for an additional 5 minutes. The mixture will thicken and develop a jamlike consistency.
3. Remove from the heat. As the compote cools, it will continue to thicken. Once cooled, transfer to a clean glass jar or container.

NOTE: *You can try this compote with different types of berries, too!*

33. Strawberry Top Smoothie

Strawberries are a close second on my favorite fruit list. Most people cut the tops off their strawberries, but strawberry leaves or strawberry greens are entirely edible. Although they are not as commonly consumed as the fruit itself, they can be eaten. Some people enjoy eating the whole berry and find the leaves to have a mild flavor. Other people find the leaves to be fibrous and slightly bitter. It's worth trying at least once, because you might like it!

Strawberry greens are often used in herbal teas and infusions. I like to eat the tops in both smoothies and salads. When making a summer strawberry salad, I quarter my strawberries with the tops still on. Between the berries and the lettuce, you won't even notice they're there. When making a smoothie, you can save yourself a lot of time by tossing the berries whole into the blender so the leafy tops are included. You can't taste them. Here's one of my favorite post-workout drinks in the summer.

MAKES 1 SMOOTHIE

10 strawberries, washed, with
    their tops
1 frozen banana

1 scoop vegan protein powder
1 cup soy milk

1. Combine all the ingredients in a blender.
2. Blend until smooth.
3. Pour into a glass and enjoy!

34. Strawberry Top Simple Syrup

I'm not crazy about eating strawberry tops raw, and still cut them off when I'm making a bowl of berries. Afterward, I still have lots of strawberry tops, but instead of composting them, I like to use them to make a delicious strawberry-infused simple syrup for a summer cocktail. You can freeze the tops if you're not ready to use them right away.

MAKES APPROXIMATELY 1 CUP

1 cup water
1 cup sugar

Tops from a 16-ounce box
of strawberries

1. Combine the water, sugar, and strawberry tops in a small saucepan over medium heat and stir gently until the sugar dissolves into the water.
2. Lower the heat and bring to a simmer. Cook for about 10 minutes, to infuse the syrup with the strawberry flavor. After 10 minutes, remove from the heat and let the syrup cool to room temperature.
3. Once cooled, strain the strawberry syrup and remove any leftover strawberry solids (you can rinse the solids and then compost them).
4. Transfer the syrup to a clean jar. The simple syrup will keep in the fridge for 2 to 3 weeks.

NOTE: *I like to use this strawberry simple syrup for a few different drinks:*

A TWIST ON THE FRENCH 75: *Use your strawberry simple syrup and garnish with a slice of strawberry instead of a twist of lemon.*

ICED STRAWBERRY GREEN TEA: *This is one of my favorite drinks to enjoy on the deck during summer afternoons. Brew a cup of green tea and let it chill. Add ice to a glass, and then add your simple syrup. You can also add a bit of muddled strawberries to up the flavor, if desired.*

STRAWBERRY LEMONADE: *You'll definitely want some muddled strawberries in this one. Combine your muddled strawberries and simple syrup with fresh lemon juice. Pour the mixture over ice in a glass. I fill mine about halfway and then top with sparkling water.*

35. Strawberry Top Vinegar

If you have a lot of strawberries, use the tops to make this vinegar that works great for salad dressings, marinades, sauces, and reductions.

MAKES APPROXIMATELY 2 CUPS

1 cup vinegar, such as
    Homemade Apple Scrap
    Vinegar (page 84), with
    the mother*

1 cup water
1 to 2 cups strawberry tops

1. Place your strawberry tops in a mason jar. Add your vinegar with the mother and your water, making sure the strawberries are fully submerged. Cover the jar with a clean cloth, using a rubber band to secure the cloth around the mouth of the jar.
2. Let the jar sit in a cabinet for 2 weeks. Then, strain the strawberry tops from the vinegar, reserving the liquid in the jar. Re-cover the jar with the cloth and let sit in the cabinet for several more weeks. The longer the jar sits, the stronger the vinegar will become.

NOTE: *The vinegar should NOT grow mold; if it has, the batch has gone bad. This can happen because a piece of fruit wasn't fully submerged. Pay attention to the smell, as well, which should be bright and pleasant—never rotten.*

---

* A vinegar mother is a viscous, gelatinous substance composed of bacteria and yeast. Healthy homemade vinegars should grow them, but you can also buy vinegar with the mother.

36. Mushy Raspberry Jam

I feel that blackberries and blueberries are the heartiest of berries. They tend to hold up fairly well. Strawberries are in the middle, but raspberries—they're fragile. Even if you handle them with care, they're still prone to turn into mush. With their delicate sensibility, raspberries should be eaten quickly. But if you've let your raspberries sit in the fridge too long, don't be dismayed. You can turn them into a quick jam perfect for thumbprint cookies, adding to yogurt, or using in a PB&J sandwich. I don't know how many leftover berries you have, but luckily this recipe is very flexible. so don't be afraid to experiment if you have fewer or more berries.

MAKES APPROXIMATELY 1 CUP JAM

1 cup mushy berries

1 tablespoon chia seeds

1 tablespoon pure maple syrup

Squeeze of fresh lemon juice

1. Place your raspberries in a saucepan over medium heat.
2. Mash the raspberries with a wooden spoon.
3. Once they're nice and bubbly, stir in the chia seeds and maple syrup, adjusting the amount to taste. The chia seeds will absorb some of the liquid and thicken the jam as it cools.
4. Continue to cook the mixture for about 5 minutes.
5. Remove from the heat and stir in the lemon juice. Taste the jam and adjust the sweetness or acidity, if desired.
6. Allow the jam to cool for a few minutes before serving or storing. As the jam cools, it will continue to thicken.
7. Store in the refrigerator for up to 1 week.

37. Cranberry Fruit Roll-Ups

Cranberry sauce isn't an especially common condiment. So, it winds up being one of the most wasted items after Thanksgiving. If you have some leftover, try blending it and then turning it into a fruit leather. You can slice the leather into large strips, or lean into childhood nostalgia and make a long, skinny fruit roll-up. It's not very practical to store them that way, but it sure is fun to eat!

SERVES 8

1 cup leftover cranberry sauce
1 apple (unpeeled),
   cored and diced
Pure maple syrup (optional)

1. Preheat your oven to 185°F. Place your cranberry sauce and the diced apple in a blender. Blend on high speed until you achieve a supersmooth puree. If the mixture is too thick, you can add a few tablespoons of water to help with blending. Add the water slowly, 1 tablespoon at a time, until you reach the desired consistency. Be careful not to add too much liquid, as you want the puree to be smooth but not watery.
2. Line a baking sheet with compostable parchment paper. Pour the cranberry mixture onto the parchment paper and use a spatula to spread it as thinly and even as possible. Aim for a thickness of around ⅛ inch.

3. Bake for approximately 5 hours. It should start to peel away from the edges. Then, turn off the oven and leave the fruit leather inside overnight. This allows the moisture to further evaporate and helps in achieving a desirable texture.

4. In the morning, check the fruit leather for a firm yet pliable consistency. It should be dry to the touch and easily peel off the parchment paper. If it feels sticky or damp, it may need additional drying time.

5. Once ready, cut the fruit leather into thin strips, and roll it up with the parchment paper intact.

6. Store the cranberry fruit roll-ups in an airtight container. They can be kept at room temperature for 2 to 3 weeks. Enjoy as a healthy snack or pack it for on-the-go treats.

NOTE: *You can use this recipe with any mushy berries. Try with blueberries, strawberries, or even both together! This recipe would also work well in a dehydrator, if you have one. If you do not properly dehydrate the berries, then moisture will get into the storage container and the roll-ups will go bad very quickly.*

38. Cranberry Sauce Muffins

When I have guests over for Thanksgiving, I like to make cranberry sauce muffins for breakfast the next morning. It's a delicious and festive way to ensure this ingredient doesn't go to waste.

MAKES 12 MUFFINS

5 tablespoons + 1 teaspoon softened vegan butter, at room temperature

½ cup brown sugar

1 cup oat flour

1½ cups all-purpose flour

1 teaspoon baking powder

¾ teaspoon baking soda

¼ teaspoon salt

1 teaspoon ground cinnamon

1½ cups milk, such as almond milk

1 flax egg (1 tablespoon ground flaxseeds mixed with 3 tablespoons water)

1 teaspoon pure vanilla extract

1¼ cups cranberry sauce

1. Preheat the oven to 400°F and line a 12-well muffin tin with liners. I use reusable silicone ones and grease them with olive oil from a refillable mist.
2. Cream together the butter and brown sugar in a large bowl until well combined.
3. Add the milk, flax egg, and vanilla. Mix until thoroughly incorporated.
4. Whisk together the oat flour, all-purpose flour, baking powder, baking soda, salt, and cinnamon in a small bowl.
5. Gradually add the flour mixture to the milk mixture, mixing until just combined. Be careful not to overmix the batter.
6. Gently fold the cranberry sauce into the batter.

7. Divide the batter evenly among the prepared muffin liners, filling each about two-thirds full.
8. Bake for approximately 20 minutes, or until a toothpick inserted into the center of a muffin comes out clean.
9. Remove from the oven and allow the muffins to cool in the tin for a few minutes before transferring them to a wire rack to cool completely.
10. Once cooled, enjoy these delicious cranberry sauce muffins as a delightful treat or for breakfast.

39. More Creative Ways to Use Cranberry Sauce

If you're still left with extra cranberry sauce, here are a few more ways you can use up this popular ingredient:

- Mix some cranberry sauce with frosting to make festive cinnamon rolls.
- Try a tart cherry and cranberry smoothie.
- Use as a sandwich spread.
- Fold into cheesecake.
- Drizzle over pound cake.

CITRUS

To maximize your citrus fruit and its flavor, store it on the countertop. For preservation and longevity, you should store it in your refrigerator. Unfortunately, cold lemons and limes produce less juice compared to those at room temperature. The cold inhibits the activity of the juice sacs within the fruit. When the fruit is warmer, the juice sacs are more active and yield more juice.

Try a few of these tips to get the most out of your citrus:

- Pull your lemons or limes out of the refrigerator so they can sit at room temperature for an hour or two before juicing them. This will help them warm up slightly and become juicier.
- Apply gentle pressure to the fruit by rolling it on a hard surface or giving it a light massage with your hands. This helps break down the inner membranes and release more juice.
- If you need to extract juice from a cold lemon or lime quickly, you can microwave it for a few seconds (10 to 15 seconds). Be careful not to overdo it, as microwaving for too long can affect the taste and texture of the fruit.

40. Use Your Citrus Peels

Citrus fruit peels are completely edible and made up of two parts. The bright colorful outside is the zest, and then the white part is known as the pith. The pith can have a strong and bitter taste, but the level of bitterness varies among different citrus varieties and individual preference. However, despite their bitterness, the whole peel can be used as flavorings, garnishes, or ingredients in different recipes.

When using citrus peels, wash the fruits thoroughly to remove any wax or pesticide residue, and if consuming the peels, try to opt for organic.

Here are a few ways you can utilize citrus peels beyond composting:

Zest: The colorful zest can be grated or chopped finely and added to dishes for a burst of citrus flavor. I recommend zesting your citrus fruits before juicing them. Spread out the zest on a pan to let it air-dry overnight. The zest will stay fresh for about two weeks in an airtight container in the fridge. You can also freeze it to incorporate into baked goods, dressings, marinades, and desserts.

Infusions: Citrus peels can be used to infuse their flavors into liquids, such as syrups, oils, or spirits. The peels are added to the liquid and left to steep, transferring their aromatic qualities. I personally like to infuse my whole citrus peels with vinegar (see Tip 43 on page 117). It makes a wonderful cleaning solution.

Candied Peels: Citrus peels can be candied by simmering them in a sugar syrup until they become tender and sweet. Candied citrus peels are often used as toppings for cakes and desserts or enjoyed as a stand-alone treat. (See Tip 41 on page 114 for how to candy peels.)

Cooking: Citrus peels can be added to stews, soups, or sauces to enhance flavor. They can be removed before serving or left in for added aroma. Just make sure you remove the pith before adding, because it can impart a bitter flavor.

41. Candied Citrus Peels

Citrus is most abundant during the late fall, winter, and early spring, making these fruits perfect for the holiday season. Dehydrated orange slices or such shapes as stars cut from just the peels are popular decorations. You can add them to colorful garlands with cranberries, popcorn, and pine branches, or string them up alone as ornaments. Beyond just decoration, these candied citrus peels also make a delicious holiday treat and are perfect in a little jar to give out as homemade gifts.

Citrus fruits, such as oranges, lemons, or grapefruits	**Water**
	Sugar

NOTE: *Grapefruit is by far the most bitter of the peels and piths, so proceed with caution. You may need to repeat the blanching process a few more times before candying.*

1. Wash the citrus peels thoroughly to remove any dirt or residue. (See Tip 19 on page 70 for washing instructions.)
2. Using a sharp knife, cut the skin of the citrus fruits into vertical strips about ¼ inch thick. Try not to get too much of the pith. It's okay if you get some, because the blanching process will reduce the bitterness.
3. Place the citrus peels in a saucepan and cover with water. Bring the water to a boil and let the peels simmer for about 5 minutes.
4. Drain the peels and repeat the boiling process one more time. This step is important to ensure the peels are soft-

ened and ready for candying. (You can keep this water for your garden.) After the second boiling, drain the peels and set aside.

5. In the same saucepan, combine sugar and water, each equal to the volume of the boiled peels. For example, if you have 1 cup of citrus peels, use 1 cup of sugar and 1 cup of water. Stir the sugar and water together over medium heat until the sugar dissolves completely. Once the sugar has dissolved, bring the mixture to a simmer over medium heat.

6. Add the citrus peels to the simmering syrup and cook them for 30 to 45 minutes, or until soft.

7. Once the peels are candied to your desired texture, remove them from the syrup, using a slotted spoon or spatula, and let them cool on a wire rack. Alternatively, you can place them on a baking sheet lined with compostable parchment paper, to dry. For an optional extra touch, you can roll the cooled candied peels in sugar, to coat them.

8. Allow the candied citrus peels to dry completely. This can take several hours to overnight.

9. Once dry, store the candied citrus peels in an airtight container. They can be enjoyed as a sweet treat on their own or used as a topping for desserts, cakes, cookies, or even added to cocktails for 2 to 3 weeks.

42. Preserved Lemons

After I've made Wilted Herb Cubes (page 152), I normally have a lot of leftover lemon peels. I like to use them to make this delicious recipe. As a warning, lemon peels can be a little bitter, and this is a very salty recipe due to the preserving process. If desired, you can rinse the preserved lemon rinds before using them in recipes, to reduce the saltiness, but keep that in mind when thinking about salt content in whatever recipe you're making.

MAKES APPROXIMATELY 1 CUP

4 to 5 lemons

¼ cup vegetable oil

¼ cup kosher salt

1. Thoroughly wash the lemons to remove any dirt or residue. Carefully peel the rinds from the lemons, trying to avoid including too much of the white pith, as it can be bitter.
2. Place the lemon rinds in a pot of boiling water and cook for about 30 minutes, or until the peels have softened.
3. Transfer the rinds to a bowl, and allow them to cool slightly.
4. Pour the vegetable oil and kosher salt over the lemon rinds, ensuring they are evenly coated.
5. Transfer to a clean, airtight container, such as a glass jar. Seal the container tightly and store it in the refrigerator. Preserved lemons can be stored like this for several weeks developing more flavor over time.

43. Lemon Peel Vinegar Cleaner

If preserved lemons aren't up your alley, try this simple home-made cleaner. It involves my favorite thing—vinegar. (I did warn you that there would be a few vinegar recipes in this book!) This recipe is perfect if you don't like the smell of vinegar, as the citrus peels mask the smell, making it much more pleasant. This cleaner is supereffective at removing soap scum, hard water stains, calcium deposits, lime, and rust.

Lemon peels
Vinegar, such as Homemade
    Apple Scrap Vinegar
    (page 84)

1. Place your lemon peels in a jar. Fill the jar half with vinegar and half with water.
2. Fasten a cloth over the top, using a rubber band, and let the jar sit in a cool, dark place, such as your pantry, for a week. Then, strain the lemon peels from the vinegar, reserving the liquid.
3. Pour the liquid into a spray bottle and it's ready to use for cleaning!

NOTE: *Lemon-infused vinegar is a natural and effective cleaner that can be used for various cleaning purposes around the house. I typically avoid using lemon-infused vinegar on mirrors and glass because the natural oils can cause streaks, and on delicate surfaces like marble or natural stone, as the acidity may cause damage.*

TOMATOES

The age-old question: Does the tomato belong in the fruit section or the vegetable section? I asked my husband what he thought and he said fruit, so that's where we ended up. When Justin and I first moved to California, we tried to grow tomatoes in our back-yard. We got three 5-gallon buckets and three Roma tomato plants. I had very high hopes. I watered the plants, got cages, and took loving care of my plant babes. By the end of the summer, we produced 2 cups of quarter-size baby tomatoes. I was quite disap-pointed in the harvest, but at least they tasted good. However, if you wind up with a bumper crop, you might be wondering, *Can I eat a soft and shriveled tomato?* Yes, you absolutely can!

Tomatoes should be stored on the counter for optimal flavor, but they last much longer in the fridge. I like to embrace a hybrid method by leaving my tomatoes on the counter and, once they're getting a little too wrinkly, I pop them in the fridge to extend their life for a few more days.

44. Shriveled Tomato Bake

This is one of my absolute favorite fast dinners, inspired by a viral TikTok recipe. If you have a pint of cherry tomatoes that's starting to go bad, you'll definitely want to make this. Shriveled tomatoes are perfect for this recipe because you're going to be shriveling them further when baking and concentrating the juice to make them sweeter.

SERVES 4

1 serving Tofu Feta
  (recipe follows)
1 pint cherry tomatoes
1 tablespoon olive oil
Salt and freshly ground
  black pepper
1 head garlic, cut in half

crosswise, exposing the top
  of the cloves
14 ounces dried pasta,
  cooked according to the
  package instructions
Pinch of red pepper
  flakes (optional)

1. Preheat your oven to 400°F. Place the tofu feta in the center of a large baking dish.
2. Arrange cherry tomatoes around the tofu in the dish. Then, drizzle the olive oil over the tomatoes and feta, and sprinkle with salt to taste.
3. Drizzle each garlic head half with olive oil and, for a zero-waste alternative to aluminum foil, place each half, face-down, in the middle of a silicone baking cup. Place each silicone-covered garlic in the corner of the baking dish.
4. Bake for 30 to 35 minutes, until the tomatoes are slightly wrinkled and bubbling. Remove the roasted garlic and

let cool for a few minutes before squeezing the garlic cloves into a small bowl. Mash the cloves, then transfer the mashed garlic back to the baking dish, along with the cooked pasta.

5. Toss the cooked pasta with the tofu feta, garlic, and tomatoes until everything is evenly combined. Add more salt and black pepper to taste, and garnish with red pepper flakes (if using), Serve hot.

Tofu Feta

7 ounces (half of a 14-ounce block) firm tofu

1 tablespoon miso paste

1 tablespoon nutritional yeast

1 tablespoon olive oil

1 teaspoon vinegar, such as Homemade Apple Scrap Vinegar (page 84)

Squeeze of fresh lemon juice

Salt and freshly ground black pepper

Dried oregano

1. Drain the tofu and place it in a food processor with all the other ingredients, adding salt, pepper, and oregano to taste.

2. Process until everything is fully incorporated and smooth. (You can add a tablespoon of water, if necessary, to achieve your desired consistency, but the water content of the tofu should be enough). When the tofu has reached your desired consistency, it's ready to add to your favorite recipe!

45. Blender Salsa

My suitemate in college used to make blender salsa all the time, and it's the perfect way to use up shriveled tomatoes. I prefer my salsa on the spicier side so I use two jalapeños and leave the seeds intact. If you want a mild salsa, simply remove the seeds.

MAKES 2 TO 3 CUPS

5 to 6 overripe tomatoes
½ cup diced red onion
¼ cup chopped fresh cilantro
2 garlic cloves, minced

1 to 2 jalapeño peppers
Juice of 1 lime
1 teaspoon ground cumin
Salt

1. Prepare the tomatoes: Cut them in half horizontally and gently squeeze out the seeds and excess juice. This will help reduce the water content and prevent the salsa from becoming too watery. Once you've seeded the tomatoes, chop them roughly.
2. Combine the chopped tomatoes, red onion, cilantro, garlic, jalapeño, lime juice, cumin, and salt in a blender or food processor. Blend until well combined, but be careful not to overblend, as that can release more liquid from the tomatoes.
3. Taste the salsa and add more salt, lime juice, or spices, according to your preference.
4. Transfer the salsa to a bowl and let sit for 15 to 30 minutes to allow the flavors to develop. Then, serve with your favorite chips.

WATERMELON

Did you know that watermelon rinds are edible? While watermelon flesh is the most commonly eaten part, the rind has its own unique texture and flavor. Watermelon rinds are often used in various culinary preparations, such as pickling, stir-frying, or even blending into smoothies or juices. When using watermelon rinds, it's important to remove the tough outer green skin. The remaining light green or white part of the rind can then be sliced, diced, or cooked according to the desired recipe.

46. Watermelon Rind Pickles

You have to serve pickled watermelon rinds at your next barbecue. I prefer mine chopped into matchsticks because they make a perfect condiment for sandwiches, burgers, hot dogs, and even tacos. They add a nice little summery, acidic crunch! These pickles are meant to be stored in the refrigerator and consumed within 2 to 3 weeks.

MAKES APPROXIMATELY 2 CUPS

3 cups peeled and cut watermelon rind (sliced into matchsticks)

1 cup vinegar, such as Strawberry Top Vinegar (page 104)

1 cup water

½ cup sugar

1 tablespoon salt

1 teaspoon whole cloves

1 teaspoon mustard seeds

1 cinnamon stick

1. Place the watermelon rind in a large bowl and sprinkle with salt. Let sit for about an hour to draw out any excess moisture. Transfer to a colander, rinse the salted watermelon rind under cold water, and drain well.

2. Combine the vinegar, water, sugar, salt, cloves, mustard seeds, and cinnamon stick in a large saucepan. Bring to a boil, stirring until the sugar is dissolved.

3. Add the watermelon rind to the boiling liquid. Lower the heat to low and simmer for 10 to 15 minutes, until the rind becomes slightly tender but still retains some crunch.

4. Remove from the heat and let the pickles cool in the liquid for about 30 minutes.

5. Transfer the pickles, along with their liquid, to a clean, sterilized jar. Make sure the pickles are completely submerged in the liquid. Cover and refrigerate for at least 24 hours before serving. The pickles will continue to develop flavor over time.

47. Watermelon Rind Jelly

While the last recipe is great for peak summer season, this recipe is perfect to bridge the gap between summer and fall. My favorite way to eat watermelon rind jelly is on fluffy biscuits, in peanut butter and jelly sandwiches, or by pouring it over vegan vanilla ice cream. The watermelon rind jelly should be consumed within a few weeks and kept refrigerated.

MAKES APPROXIMATELY 1 CUP JELLY

4 cups peeled watermelon rinds

1 apple, peeled and diced (the natural pectin in the apple will help set the jelly)

½ cup sugar

Juice of 1 lemon

1 teaspoon pure vanilla extract

Pinch of salt

1. Combine the peeled rinds, apple cubes, sugar, lemon juice, vanilla, and salt in a large saucepan. Bring the mixture to a boil over medium heat, stirring occasionally as it warms.
2. Once the liquid reaches a boil, lower the heat to low and cover the saucepan. Simmer for about an hour, or until the watermelon rinds and apple have softened.
3. Remove from the heat and let cool. Then blend until smooth.
4. Store the watermelon rind jelly in a jar or airtight container in the refrigerator for up to 2 weeks and enjoy in your favorite recipes.

CHAPTER 4

SAVING YOUR VEGGIES

Beyond just peak produce, we need to talk about the untapped potential of less commonly used vegetable scraps. There's a lot that we can eat but don't. Many people throw out broccoli stalks, carrot and leek tops, potato peels, and more, but they're bursting with flavor if you know how to use them.

Broccoli stalks are incredibly tender and delicious once you peel away that rough outer layer. Carrot tops are actually in the same family as parsley; they're a touch sweeter than parsley but can be used as a one-to-one substitute in almost all recipes. You can save those leek tops for a delicious veggie scrap broth and turn those potato peels into a crunchy chip-like snack.

In this chapter, we'll dive in to food recipes using vegetables that are visually or texturally past their prime, and find new culinary life for the less-popular scraps like stalks and tops.

BROCCOLI

I grew up in a house where everyone spent their time in the kitchen. Both my parents loved to cook and were excellent at it. As a result, I loved my vegetables while growing up. Green beans are the front-runner in my list of favorites, but broccoli is a pretty close second. So, imagine my surprise to learn that most people in the United States throw out their broccoli stalks! Turn the page for how to make the most of your broccoli stalks.

48. Roasted Broccoli Florets and Stalks

At the grocery store, most broccoli is sold per pound. If you throw out the stalk, you're wasting more than half your money. More than that, you're missing out on perfectly good food. Broccoli stalks are just as delicious as the florets if you prepare them properly. The secret is to peel away the outermost layer. It can be really thick and fibrous, but once it is removed, you'll find a super-tender interior that can roast on a baking sheet with the rest of your florets. I think they look the best and cook evenly when cut into matchsticks.

I use all of my seasonings to taste and just eyeball it based on what I'm feeling. Do what works best for you!

SERVES 4 TO 6

1 bunch broccoli	Dried basil
1 tablespoon olive oil	Salt and freshly ground
Garlic powder	black pepper
Nutritional yeast	Crushed red pepper flakes

1. Preheat your oven to 400°F.
2. Cut the broccoli florets off the stalks, reserving the stalks, and chop the florets into bite-size pieces. Then, cut off the very bottom of the broccoli stalks. Peel away the roughest outer layer of the stalks and discard the peels for compost. Cut the remaining tender stalks into matchstick-size pieces.

3. Place the florets and stalks on a baking sheet. Drizzle them with the olive oil and season to taste with garlic powder, nutritional yeast, dried basil, salt, black pepper, and crushed red pepper flakes. Toss the broccoli pieces gently on the pan to evenly coat them with the oil and seasonings, then spread them out in a single layer.

4. Roast in the oven for approximately 20 minutes, or until tender and golden. Enjoy in salads, bowls, and more!

BEET GREENS

Although often thrown out, beet tops, also known as beet greens or beet leaves, are edible and nutritious. They're the leafy greens that grow above the ground on beet plants. They're rich in vitamins A, C, and K, as well as such minerals as iron, calcium, and potassium.

If you've ever bought beets with the tops, you might have noticed they look a *lot* like chard. That's because both beet tops and chard belong to the same plant family, Chenopodiaceae. In fact, chard is often referred to as "leaf beet" or "Swiss chard beet" due to its close resemblance to beet tops.

In terms of taste and culinary use, both beet tops and chard have a similar earthy and slightly bitter flavor. The leaves of both plants can be cooked and used interchangeably in recipes. The main difference is that chard stems are often more pronounced, colorful, and tender, whereas beet-top stems can be a bit tougher and more fibrous.

When cooking beet tops, it's best to separate the leaves from the stems, as the stems can be tougher and take longer to cook. However, both the leaves and stems are edible and can be used in different ways.

49. Roasted Beet Green Salad

If you buy beets with their stems attached, it's basically like getting chard for free! So, while not exactly the same, they're so closely related they can be used in similar ways for cooking. You can try them sautéed, steamed, boiled, or added to soups and stews. But I love adding them raw to salads like this one.

MAKES 4 SMALL SIDE SALADS

Olive oil for baking dish
   and tossing
3 medium beets with stems
   and leaves
Salt and freshly ground
   black pepper

2 clementines, peeled and
   separated into segments
¼ cup pistachios, almonds, or
   walnuts, chopped
Balsamic glaze for drizzling

1. Preheat the oven to 400°F and oil a baking dish.
2. Scrub the beets clean and trim away any roots. Separate the greens from the beets and set them aside. Place the beets in your baking dish and tent it. Often you tent pans with foil, but I like to use a baking dish with a cookie sheet on top. It results in the same effect without the waste!
3. Roast the beets in the oven for 45 to 60 minutes, or until they are tender and able to be pierced with a fork.
4. While the beets are roasting, prepare the stems: Separate the beet stems from the leaves, reserving the leaves, and chop the stems into small pieces. Place the stems in a medium bowl and toss with a little oil, salt, and pepper,

then add them to the baking dish during the last 10 minutes of roasting.

5. Remove the beets and stems from the oven and let them cool. Once they are at room temperature, you can peel the skin off the beets. Discard and compost the peels, then dice the beets into bite-size pieces.

6. Arrange the beet leaves in a serving bowl as the base of the salad. Top them with the roasted beets and stems. Sprinkle the clementines and nuts over the salad and toss gently to combine all the ingredients. Finish with the balsamic glaze and serve.

CABBAGE

Cabbage is often cited as one of the most wasted produce items. It's not considered very versatile and many recipes only call for half or a quarter of the vegetable, resulting in the other half going to waste. Let's avoid this!

50. Roasted Cabbage

If you find yourself with leftover cabbage, you have to try this roasted cabbage salad. It's one of my favorite recipes in the book. Add a generous heaping of dressing and top with crispy roasted chickpeas or add in quinoa.

MAKES 3 OR 4 SERVINGS

½ cabbage
1 to 2 tablespoons olive oil
Salt and freshly ground
  black pepper
Garlic powder

1 bunch lacinato kale
2 to 3 tablespoons miso paste
Juice of 1 to 2 lemons
Pure maple syrup

1. Preheat your oven to 400°F.
2. Shred the cabbage into thin strips. Arrange the cabbage shreds in a single layer on a baking sheet, drizzle them with olive oil, then season to taste with salt, pepper, and garlic powder. Roast in the oven for about 30 minutes, or until golden brown.
3. While the cabbage is roasting, chop your lacinato kale into small strips. During the last 10 minutes of roasting, add your kale to the pan.
4. To prepare the dressing, whisk together the miso paste, lemon juice, and maple syrup to taste in a small bowl until well combined. Adjust the sweetness and acidity according to your taste.
5. Remove the roasted greens from the oven and transfer to a serving dish. Drizzle the miso dressing over the roasted greens and serve.

CARROT TOPS

Carrot tops, also known as carrot greens, are my favorite food scrap of all time. Most people don't eat them and choose to throw them out, but you absolutely should enjoy them. They're perfectly edible and underutilized. Carrot tops and parsley belong to the same plant family, known as Apiaceae or Umbelliferae. This family includes a variety of plants that share similar characteristics and are often used as herbs or vegetables.

If you buy carrots with the tops at the grocery store, it's basically like getting parsley for free. Carrot tops are a touch sweeter and a little less harsh, which I find to be preferable! These commonly discarded gems add a fresh and herbaceous element to dishes, and their flavors can complement a wide range of ingredients.

51. Carrot Top Chimichurri Sauce

This chimichurri sauce is my favorite recipe in the whole book. Traditionally a popular Argentinean sauce made with parsley, garlic, olive oil, vinegar, and other herbs and spices, here it is a quick dressing inspired by chimichurri flavors. Preparation uses a blender, which you wouldn't traditionally use to make chimichurri, but it whips up superfast and I hope it will become a favorite condiment of yours, too. My favorite way to enjoy this sauce is with roasted potatoes, grilled zucchini, or a tofu breakfast scramble.

MAKES APPROXIMATELY 2 CUPS

1 shallot

1 jalapeño pepper

3 to 4 garlic cloves

1 bunch fresh oregano

1 bunch fresh cilantro

1 bunch carrot tops

½ cup red wine vinegar, such as Leftover Red Wine Vinegar (page 227)

1 cup extra-virgin olive oil

Salt and freshly ground black pepper (optional)

1. Roughly chop the shallot, jalapeño (remove the seeds for less heat, if desired), and garlic cloves. Remove and discard the oregano stems and cut off the thick ends of the cilantro stems and carrot tops. (You can compost these discarded bits.)

2. Combine the shallot, jalapeño, garlic, oregano, cilantro, carrot tops, red wine vinegar, and olive oil in a blender or food processor. Blend the ingredients until a smooth and well-combined mixture is achieved. Taste the sauce and

adjust the seasoning, if needed, by adding salt and black pepper to taste.

3. When you've achieved your desired flavor, transfer to a container or jar with a tight-fitting lid. Store the chimichurri in the refrigerator for at least 1 hour before using, to allow the flavors to meld together. Enjoy its vibrant and herbaceous flavors!

52. Carrot Top Gremolata

This gremolata is a vibrant and flavorful herb condiment that's superquick to whip up. Recently, I added it to a creamy, springlike pasta with asparagus, but my favorite way to use it is in a big broccoli bake topped with lots of homemade bread crumbs (see the Pro Tip on page 186). You can keep the sauce in an airtight container in the fridge for a little over a week.

MAKES APPROXIMATELY 1 CUP

1 cup chopped carrot
   top leaves
2 garlic cloves, minced finely
Zest and juice of 1 lemon
¼ cup olive oil

Salt and freshly ground
   black pepper
Pinch of red pepper
   flakes (optional)

Combine the carrot top leaves, garlic, lemon zest and juice, olive oil, salt, black pepper, and red pepper flakes (if using) in a medium bowl. Mix until well combined and the ingredients are evenly distributed.

> **Pro Tip:** *If you have carrots that are starting to wilt, sub them for the pumpkin in my Pumpkin Soup (page 171).*

53. More Ways to Enjoy Carrot Tops

Tabbouleh: This Middle Eastern salad typically features parsley as a key ingredient, but you can use carrot tops instead. Combine chopped carrot tops with bulgur wheat, tomatoes, cucumbers, mint, lemon juice, olive oil, and other herbs to create a refreshing salad.

Herb sauces and pesto: Like parsley, carrot greens can be combined with other herbs, such as fresh basil or cilantro, to create flavorful sauces and pesto. These herb-based sauces are versatile and can be used as a topping for pasta, grilled vegetables, or as a dip for bread.

Garnishes: You can also use the carrot tops just as a garnish or finishing touch on various dishes, adding a pop of color and freshness.

CAULIFLOWER LEAVES

At the grocery store, the cauliflower you find is often stripped of its leaves. They're trimmed for a tidier appearance and easier handling. Sometimes, a few leaves are attached, but if you grow your own cauliflower, or if you can find it at the local farmers' market, it's worth looking for a cauliflower that comes with leaves and all.

54. Roasted Cauliflower Leaves

Cauliflower leaves have a mild and slightly earthy flavor similar to that of other leafy greens. The larger outer leaves can be slightly bitter, but such cooking methods as roasting, sautéing, or steaming can help soften them and bring out their natural sweetness.

SERVES 2

Cauliflower leaves (from
1 cauliflower head)
Olive oil
Salt and freshly ground
black pepper

Optional seasonings: garlic
powder, smoked paprika,
red pepper flakes, or your
preferred spices

1. Preheat the oven to 400°F.
2. Rinse the cauliflower leaves thoroughly under cold water to remove any dirt or debris. Pat dry with a kitchen towel, then tear into bite-size pieces, discarding any tough stems for composting.
3. Place on a baking sheet. Drizzle with olive oil and sprinkle with salt, black pepper, and any additional seasonings you desire. Toss well to coat the leaves evenly, then spread them out in a single layer on the baking sheet.
4. Roast in the oven for 10 to 15 minutes, until they turn crispy and slightly browned. Keep an eye on them to prevent burning.
5. Remove from the oven and let cool slightly before serving. Enjoy as a healthy and flavorful snack, or use them as a tasty topping for salads, soups, or grain bowls.

CORN

The next time you make corn, save the cobs. Corn cobs aren't especially pleasant to eat because they're tough and fibrous, but they still have a lot of uses. In the 1800s, corn cobs would be dried and tightly packed into gaps and crevices in buildings and used as insulation material. My friend recently bought a farmhouse in Vermont, and the home was insulated with a mix of old paper and corn cobs.

But don't worry, this is a recipe book, not a renovation book! I'm not recommending that you save your corn cobs to insulate your home. But consider a few of these recipes to utilize all parts of your corn.

55. Corn Stock

This stock can be used as a base for soups (such as corn chowder), stews, a summer risotto, or in any recipe that calls for vegetable stock.

MAKES APPROXIMATELY 6 CUPS

4 to 6 corn cobs

Water

Bay leaves

Salt and freshly ground black pepper

1. Place your corn cobs, bay leaves, and salt and pepper to taste in a large pot. Add enough water to cover, then bring the water to a boil over medium-high heat.
2. Lower the heat to low and let the corn cobs simmer for 1 to 2 hours. This will extract the flavor from the cobs.
3. Remove the pot from the heat and allow the stock to cool slightly.
4. Strain the stock through a fine-mesh sieve to remove the corn cobs, reserving the liquid and saving the cobs for compost.
5. Let the stock cool completely before transferring it to storage containers. Store the corn stock in the refrigerator for up to 3 to 4 days, or freeze it for up to 3 months.

56. Corn Cob Jelly

Corn cob jelly or corn cob preserves is an old canning recipe that I stumbled upon. From what I can gather, it originated in the United States. It gained popularity in the early 20th century in farming communities as a means of making the most of the corn harvest.

By boiling corn cobs in water and extracting the natural pectin, a jelly-like consistency could be achieved. This jelly was then flavored with sugar, lemon juice, and sometimes other ingredients to create a sweet and tangy spread. I think it tastes a lot like honey. I like to spread mine on toast with peanut butter or drizzle it over biscuits.

MAKES APPROXIMATELY 1 CUP

2 corn cobs

2 cups water

½ cup sugar

1 tablespoon cornstarch

1 tablespoon cold water

Pinch of ground
    turmeric (optional)

1. Cut your corn cobs in half crosswise and place them in a small saucepan along with the water.
2. Bring the water to a simmer over medium heat, cover, and let cook for about 15 minutes to extract the flavor from the cobs. Keep the lid on to prevent too much evaporation.
3. Strain the liquid from the saucepan through a fine-mesh sieve or cheesecloth. Save the cobs for composting.
4. Return the broth to the saucepan and place back over medium heat. Add the sugar.

5. Stir together the cornstarch with cold water in a small bowl, to create a slurry.

6. Gradually add the slurry to the simmering corn cob broth, stirring continuously to prevent lumps from forming. For a touch of color, you can add a pinch of turmeric to the mixture at this stage and stir well.

7. Continue to heat over medium heat, stirring constantly, until thickened. This usually takes about 2 minutes. Once the sauce has reached your desired consistency, remove from the heat.

8. Allow the corn cob jelly to cool slightly before using or storing in an airtight container.

57. More Ways to Use All Parts of Your Corn

Tamales: Corn husks are commonly used in making tamales. The husks are soaked and filled with masa (a corn-based dough) and various fillings. Then, they're steamed in the husk which provides a natural wrapping for the tamale.

Tea: The fine threads found inside the corn husks, known as corn silk, can be used to make a soothing tea. It has a lightly sweet and earthy flavor. The taste can vary depending on the freshness of the corn silk, so you may want to add maple syrup, lemon, or herbs to enhance it.

CUCUMBERS

Of all the items in this book, cucumbers are the ones I struggle with the most. They seem to go bad so quickly. They have a high moisture content and thin skin, so even if they've been stored properly, they should be eaten within a couple of days. But if you end up losing out on fresh cucumbers, you can still utilize them for tasty dishes!

58. Cucumber Gazpacho

If your cucumbers have lost their crunch try making this refreshing gazpacho. You can adjust the consistency of the soup by adding a little water or more yogurt, if desired. As always, feel free to experiment with additional herbs or spices to personalize the flavor.

SERVES 2

1 cucumber, peeled and
chopped roughly
1 small shallot,
chopped roughly
1 cup plain plant-based yogurt
1 tablespoon olive oil, plus
more for serving
1 tablespoon minced mint

1 tablespoon minced fresh
parsley or carrot tops, plus
more for serving
1 tablespoon dill pickle juice or
sherry vinegar
Juice of 1 lemon
Salt

1. Combine the cucumber, shallot, yogurt, olive oil, mint, parsley, and dill pickle juice in a blender. Blend until smooth and creamy.
2. Season with the lemon juice and salt to taste, adjusting the flavors to your liking.
3. Transfer the soup to a container and refrigerate for at least 1 hour to chill.
4. Before serving, garnish with minced parsley and a drizzle of olive oil.

HERBS

I have always wanted an herb garden. Nothing elevates a dish quite like fresh herbs, but I have tried and failed several times at growing some of the classics, such as basil, cilantro, and mint. Herbs from the grocery store can be expensive and often come in plastic clamshells. If you have a green thumb, it's definitely worth growing them! If you don't, like me, let's make sure we utilize every last leaf and stem.

59. Use Herb Stems

Although woody herb stems, such as those from rosemary, thyme, and oregano, are usually not palatable, there are other herbs whose stems are completely delicious. Some herb stems, such as cilantro and parsley stems, are tender and flavorful, and they can be chopped or blended, and then used along with the leaves in various dishes. If you're ever unsure about whether you can use herb stems, it's always a good idea to taste the stems and assess their texture and flavor before deciding whether to include them in your dish. Even if you can't chop them and eat them raw, herb stems are often full of flavor, so consider tying them in a bundle and adding to Homemade Vegetable Stock (page 175).

60. Wilted Herb Cubes

When stored properly, most of your fresh herbs will last for about a week, but it can still be challenging to eat the whole bunch in a week. So, I started making herb cubes. (The cilantro-lime herb cubes are my favorite!) When using the frozen herb cubes, simply remove as many cubes as needed for your recipe and thaw them as necessary. The herbs can be added directly to soups, stews, sauces, or other dishes while cooking.

Fresh herbs of your choice, chopped finely

Oil (such as olive oil), water, lemon juice, lime juice (or other desired liquid)

1. Fill each compartment of an ice cube tray with the chopped herbs, distributing them evenly.
2. Choose your desired medium for freezing the herbs. You can opt for oil, water, lemon juice, lime juice, or any other liquid that complements your herbs. Pour the chosen medium over the herbs in each compartment, ensuring they are fully covered.
3. Carefully transfer the filled ice cube tray to the freezer. Freeze the herbs until solid, typically for a few hours or overnight.
4. Once frozen, remove the herb cubes from the tray and transfer them to a freezer-safe container or bag. Label the container or bag with the herb variety and enjoy as needed.

KALE

Like most greens, kale should be eaten quickly before it begins to wilt. However, if you can't eat your kale when it's fresh, there are plenty of ways to make the most of it past its prime.

61. Give It an Ice Bath

Last year, I needed lacinato kale for a recipe. Lacinato kale is the superior kale and no one can change my mind. My local produce stand only had one bunch left and it was looking rough. It was pretty droopy. In fact, it was so droopy that the lady at the checkout counter gave it to me for free.

When I got home, I cut about 2 inches off the bottom stems and put the kale into an ice bath. I let it soak for about 20 minutes, and when I pulled it out, it was revived to its former glory. It was even crunchy again! Then, I stored it like a bouquet of flowers—upright in a mason jar—in the fridge.

This ice bath hack works with a lot of different vegetables to give you just an extra day or two of crispiness. (If, however, a vegetable is clearly disintegrating and smells bad, send it straight to compost.)

62. Pasta with Lemon-Kale Sauce

If you need to use some wilting kale, try making this delicious and springlike pasta sauce.

SERVES 4

1 bunch kale, stems removed, leaves chopped

One 1-pound box dried pasta of your choice

Juice of 1 lemon

¼ cup extra-virgin olive oil, plus 1 tablespoon and more for finishing

Salt and freshly ground black pepper

2 shallots

4 garlic cloves

Lemon zest

Vegan Parmesan (see Pro Tip)

1. Bring a large pot of salted water to a boil. Add the kale leaves and blanch for 2 to 3 minutes, until tender, and pull them out, using tongs, and transfer to an ice bath, leaving the blanching liquid in the pot. Drain the kale and set it aside.

2. In the same pot, in the reserved salted water, cook the pasta according to the package instructions until almost al dente. Drain the cooked pasta, reserving ⅓ to ½ a cup of the cooking water.

3. Combine the blanched kale, lemon juice, olive oil, and ⅓ cup of the reserved pasta water in a blender or food processor. Blend until you achieve a smooth and creamy consistency. Season with salt and pepper to taste.

4. Place the pot back on the stove with a tablespoon of olive oil and sauté the shallots until translucent. Add the garlic, and once fragrant, add back the sauce and pasta.
5. If needed, add another splash of the reserved pasta water to loosen the sauce and achieve your desired consistency.
6. Serve warm and garnish with additional lemon zest, a drizzle of olive oil, and lots of vegan Parmesan.

> **Pro Tip:** *To make vegan Parmesan, blend 1 cup of cashews with ¼ cup of nutritional yeast and a pinch of salt and garlic powder.*

MUSHROOMS

Mushrooms, like cucumbers, can be a little finicky. When you get home from the store, do not wash them unless you're immediately going to eat them. Unwashed mushrooms should last in your fridge for around seven days. Mushrooms have a high water content, and they absorb water quickly. When you're ready to eat them, you can rinse them briefly under cold water and pat them dry, but make sure they're completely dry before cooking. When mushrooms absorb excess water, their flavor becomes diluted, and their texture can be rubbery and slimy when cooked. If using cultivated mushrooms, such as portobellos and button mushrooms, you can also brush off any visible dirt or debris, using a soft brush or cloth.

63. Shriveled Mushrooms

Because of their high water content, as mushrooms age, they will lose some of their perkiness and start to wrinkle. If it's coming to the end of the week with my button mushrooms and they're slightly wrinkled, I like to cook them over high heat. This helps develop a rich, savory flavor. Keep an eye on them as they cook, to prevent burning.

MAKES APPROXIMATELY 1 CUP

2 tablespoons olive oil

1 pound shriveled mushrooms, sliced

3 garlic cloves, minced

1 tablespoon soy sauce

1 tablespoon balsamic vinegar

Fresh thyme or herb of your choice, chopped (optional)

Salt and freshly ground black pepper

1. Heat a large skillet over medium-high heat and add the olive oil. Add the sliced mushrooms to the hot skillet and, using a spatula, spread them out into a single layer. Let cook undisturbed for a few minutes, until they start to brown.

2. Stir in the minced garlic and continue to cook for another minute, until fragrant.

3. Add the soy sauce and balsamic vinegar to the skillet and stir to coat the mushrooms evenly. Cook the mushrooms for a few more minutes, stirring occasionally, until they are nicely browned and tender.

4. Sprinkle with fresh herbs, if using, and season with salt and pepper to taste.

5. Remove from heat and serve as a side dish or use as a topping for pasta or sandwiches.

NOTE: *A few wrinkles are fine, but if the mushrooms appear extremely dry, or discolored, or are growing mold or smelling foul, you should probably compost them. As always, it's best to use your senses and err on the side of caution if there are any doubts about their quality.*

POTATOES

When I lived in a loft in Berkeley, the whole kitchen was open. We only had one cabinet door, and it was the door under the kitchen sink. Everything else was open shelving. I stored my potatoes in a bowl at the very far back of the shelf under the kitchen island, but they had to be eaten fast or they would start to wrinkle and sprout in under a week.

When storing your potatoes properly, they should last a lot longer than a week. But if your potatoes are starting to wrinkle and have tiny sprouts, those are indicators that they're starting to age. If the potato appears firm and healthy with a few small sprouts, removing the sprouts and using the potato in cooking should be fine. However, other signs of spoilage, such as a soft or really wrinkly texture, green discoloration, or an unpleasant odor means it's probably best to compost the potato.

64. Mashed Potato Gnocchi

I don't make mashed potatoes very often, but much like pasta, I find it very difficult to make just one serving. I always seem to have way too many mashed potatoes. If you have too many mashed potatoes, try making mashed potato gnocchi.

SERVES 2

> 1 cup mashed potatoes
> 1 cup all-purpose flour, plus
>   more for dusting
> 2 to 3 tablespoons olive oil

1. Combine the mashed potatoes and flour in a medium bowl. Add a few tablespoons of olive oil. Mix together until well combined. The dough should be slightly sticky.
2. Transfer the dough to a floured work surface or countertop. Generously sprinkle flour over the dough and knead it until you achieve a smooth and springy consistency. The dough should be elastic and not stick to your hands or the surface. If needed, add more flour gradually during the kneading process.
3. Once the dough is smooth and springy, roll it into a narrow log. Make sure the log is evenly sized about 1 inch in diameter, then gently shape it to have four equal, flat sides along its length. Slice the log into 1-inch squares.
4. Using a fork, press the tines against each dough square to create ridges and roll while pressing, to give the dough its

traditional gnocchi shape. Repeat this process for all the dough until all the squares are ridged and curved.

5. Bring a pot of salted water to a boil. Gently place the gnocchi in the boiling water and cook for 2 to 3 minutes, or until they rise to the surface.

6. Using a slotted spoon or strainer, carefully remove the cooked gnocchi from the water and transfer to a serving dish.

7. Serve the freshly cooked gnocchi with your favorite sauce or toppings.

65. Potato Peel Snacks

If you're making mashed potatoes, you probably have leftover potato peels. But don't compost them; try this crunchy snack instead. These make a great crispy topping for casseroles, or just as a snack. The cooking time may vary depending on the thickness and moisture content of the potato peels. But you can adjust the cooking time accordingly and check them periodically for desired crispness.

SERVES 1

Olive oil

Peels of 1 potato

Your favorite spices (salt, garlic, cumin, smoked paprika, etc.)

1. Preheat your oven to 425°F and oil a baking sheet well. Place the potato peels on the prepared baking sheet, then drizzle more oil over the peels, ensuring they are evenly coated. Use enough oil to lightly coat the peels, but not too much more than that.
2. Sprinkle your favorite spices over the peels. You can use a combination of salt, garlic powder, cumin, smoked paprika, or any other preferred spices for added flavor.
3. Gently toss the peels on the baking sheet, making sure they are well coated with the oil and spices.
4. Spread out the peels in a single layer on the baking sheet, to allow for even cooking. Roast in the oven for about 10 minutes, or until the peels are crispy and golden brown.

Keep a close eye on them during the last few minutes, to prevent burning.

5. Once the peels are cooked to your desired crispness, remove from the oven and let cool slightly. Enjoy as a snack or topping.

SPINACH

The best way to store spinach is in an airtight container with a small swatch of cloth on top of the leaves to absorb any excess moisture. Using this method, I've been able to keep it at peak freshness for at least two weeks. However, when it does start to wilt or a few pieces get slimy (I always pick the slimy leaves out), I like to blend it into different recipes!

66. Spinach and Basil Pesto

This spinach and basil pesto can be used as a delicious sauce for pasta, a spread for sandwiches, a topping for roasted vegetables, or as a flavorful addition to soups and salads.

MAKES APPROXIMATELY 3 CUPS

1 bunch basil (about 1½ cups)

1½ cups wilted spinach

3 to 4 garlic cloves

¼ cup olive oil

¼ cup pine nuts, cashews, or
  sunflower seeds

¼ cup nutritional yeast

Juice of 1 lemon

Salt and freshly ground
  black pepper

1. Wash the basil leaves and remove any tough stems. Wilt all the spinach further by lightly sautéing or steaming it in a pan over medium heat for a few minutes.

2. Combine the basil, wilted spinach, garlic, olive oil, nuts or seeds, nutritional yeast, and lemon juice in a blender or food processor. Blend until smooth and creamy. If needed, add a small amount of water to achieve the desired consistency. Taste the pesto and season with salt and pepper according to your preference. Adjust the flavors as desired by adding more lemon juice, garlic, or nutritional yeast.

3. Transfer the pesto to a jar or airtight container. It can be stored in the refrigerator for up to 1 week.

67. Spinach Smoothie Cubes

Smoothies are one of the few things I eat several times a week, and having frozen smoothie cubes ready to go is an easy way to add a few greens.

MAKES 1 TO 1½ ICE CUBE TRAYS OF CUBES

2 cups wilted spinach
1 cup plant-based milk, such
    as almond milk, soy milk, or
    coconut milk

1. Wilt all the spinach further by lightly sautéing or steaming it in a pan over medium heat for a few minutes.
2. Combine the wilted spinach and milk in a blender. Blend until smooth and well combined. You can add more or less milk to adjust the consistency according to your preference.
3. Pour the spinach mixture into an ice cube tray (or more than one tray if necessary), filling each compartment. Place the ice cube tray in the freezer and let the smoothie cubes freeze until solid, which typically takes 3 to 4 hours.
4. Once the smoothie cubes are fully frozen, remove from the ice cube tray and transfer to a freezer-safe container or resealable bag. Label the container with the date and contents. It will be good for about 3 months.

Whenever you're making a smoothie, simply add a few spinach smoothie cubes to the blender along with your other ingredients.

PUMPKIN

Nothing says "autumn" like a pumpkin. We decorate with them, we carve them, we lovingly pick them from patches, we take family photos with them, and then we throw them in the landfill. More than 2 billion pounds of pumpkins are grown every year for all our pumpkin needs, and according to the US Department of Energy, 1.3 billion pounds are uneaten and sent to the landfill.

So, why don't we eat them? The whole entire pumpkin is edible. Big jack-o'-lantern pumpkins are grown for size, not flavor, but they're still totally edible and delicious. Here's how I turn my porch pumpkin into dinner.

> **Pro Tip:** *I live in Maine. The weather is cool in late October. I place a fully intact pumpkin on the porch for a few days and then bring it inside for food. If you're carving your pumpkin and leaving it on the porch, eat the carved-out bits, and then compost the rest of the pumpkin after it's been outside or donate extra whole pumpkins to local farms or animal sanctuary.*

68. Pumpkin Puree

Interestingly enough, canned pumpkin often contains a combination of various winter squash varieties, such as butternut squash, which has a similar taste and texture. This puree is 100 percent pumpkin. I recommend sugar pumpkins; carving pumpkins will work, but they are less flavorful and have a higher water content.

YIELD VARIES BASED ON PUMPKIN SIZE

1 pumpkin

1. Preheat the oven to 400°F. Wash the pumpkin thoroughly to remove any dirt or debris. Using a sharp knife, cut off the stem and slice the pumpkin in half vertically.
2. Scoop out any seeds and reserve them for the next recipe. The pumpkin pulp is edible, so you can leave that inside the pumpkin halves. Place the pumpkin halves, cut side down, on a baking sheet.
3. Roast in the oven for about an hour, or until the flesh becomes tender and is easily pierced with a fork. Remove from the oven and allow to cool slightly. If you want you, can blend the skin of the pumpkin with the flesh, but if not, it's very easy to peel the roasted flesh from the skin with your hands. The flesh should be soft and easily separable.
4. Transfer the pumpkin to a food processor. Blend until smooth and creamy.
5. Store the puree in airtight containers in the refrigerator for up to 5 days or freeze for several months.

69. Spiced and Roasted Pumpkin Seeds

I love keeping pumpkin seeds around to snack on, or even to use as a topping for pumpkin soup! This is the perfect way to make use of the seeds after you carve a pumpkin or make pumpkin puree.

MAKES 2 CUPS

Seeds from 1 large pumpkin
Olive oil
Seasonings of your choice:
For sweet seeds, pumpkin
    spice blend and pure
    maple syrup

For salty seeds, salt, garlic,
    ancho chile powder,
    smoked paprika

1. Wash the pumpkin seeds and towel dry them. I like to let them sit out overnight for extra crispiness.
2. Preheat your oven to 350°F and spread out the pumpkin seeds on a baking sheet. Coat the seeds with a bit of olive oil. Sprinkle with your desired amount of the sweet or salty seasoning mixture.
3. Roast in the oven for about 15 minutes, giving them a good shake halfway through. When the seeds are toasty and a little golden, remove them from the oven and allow them to cool before enjoying.

70. Pumpkin Soup

Every fall, I use my pumpkin puree to make a savory pumpkin soup and top it with my homemade roasted pumpkin seeds and a big dollop of vegan yogurt. The curry paste makes this recipe come together in a snap.

SERVES 8

8 cups pumpkin puree

2 to 3 cups vegetable stock, such as Homemade Vegetable Stock (page 175)

2 to 3 heaping tablespoons Patak's brand mild curry paste, or your preferred curry paste

¼ cup pure maple syrup

¼ cup sherry vinegar or apple cider vinegar, such as Homemade Apple Scrap Vinegar (page 84)

Salt and freshly ground black pepper

1. Combine the pumpkin puree, vegetable broth, curry paste, maple syrup, and sherry vinegar in a large pot. Stir until well combined. Adjust the seasonings according to your taste, adding salt and pepper as desired.

2. Place the pot over medium heat and bring to a simmer. Let simmer for 15 to 20 minutes, stirring occasionally, to allow the flavors to meld together.

3. Once the soup is heated through and the flavors have developed, remove from the heat. Serve the pumpkin soup hot, garnishing with the spiced and roasted pumpkin seeds, if desired.

71. Whole Pumpkin Crackers

This was the first recipe I tried with a jack-o'-lantern pumpkin. Since jack-o'-lantern pumpkins aren't grown for their flavor, I thought I would opt for a recipe that would be nice with just a hint of pumpkin, but these crackers were amazing. It's such a creative way to use some of your pumpkin puree. As a bonus, you can share a few of these with your canine friends if you leave out the spices!

MAKES 50 TO 60 CRACKERS

1 cup of Pumpkin Puree
   (page 169)
½ cup milled flaxseeds
3 cups all-purpose flour, plus
   more for dusting

Your choice of spices (if
   making for humans;
   omit for dogs)

1. Preheat your oven to 375°F
2. Combine the pumpkin puree and milled flaxseeds in a large bowl, and let it sit for 5 minutes. While mixing, gradually add 3 cups of flour, 1 cup at a time, until a dough forms. The dough should be firm and not too sticky (I like to use a food processor). If desired and you're preparing the crackers for human consumption, add your choice of spices to the dough for additional flavor.
3. On a well-floured surface, knead the dough until it becomes smooth and well combined. Use a rolling pin to roll out the dough (approximately ⅛" inch thick). Cut the dough into your preferred shapes, using cookie cutters, and place the shaped dough ¼-inch apart on your cookie sheet.

4. Bake for about 15 minutes, or until firm and golden brown. The crackers should be crispy. Remove from the oven and let cool completely on a wire rack.

5. Once cooled, store in an airtight container for 1 week to 10 days.

VEGGIE SCRAPS (ONION SKINS, GARLIC SKINS)

Saving your vegetable ends and stems in the freezer to make homemade veggie stock is a great way to reduce waste, extract maximum flavor, and did I mention it's totally free? The next time you're prepping food, collect your onion peels, garlic peels, carrot tops/peels, and herb stems to build a stockpile of ingredients. I like to keep mine in a lidded container in the freezer.

72. Homemade Vegetable Stock

Once my scrap bin is full in the freezer, I make a homemade vegetable stock that can be used for homemade soups, such as Pumpkin Soup (page 171), and for adding depth to grains, such as rice and quinoa. I do leave out cruciferous veggies (e.g., broccoli, cauliflower, Brussels sprouts, and kale), as they can make the veggie stock bitter.

YIELD VARIES

Aromatic food scraps of your choice (garlic peels, onion peels, carrot tops/peels, celery bits, herb stems, etc.)

Water
Fresh herbs, such as thyme, rosemary, and bay leaves (optional)

1. Place your food scraps in a large pot, Instant Pot®, or slow cooker. Add enough water to cover the scraps, ensuring they are fully submerged. If desired, add your fresh herbs of choice, to enhance the flavor.
2. Simmer the mixture for 1 hour on the stovetop, for 20 minutes on HIGH in an Instant Pot, or for approximately 6 hours in a slow cooker set to HIGH. Once cooked, strain the stock through a fine-mesh sieve to remove the solids, reserving the liquid.
3. Allow the stock to cool completely before storing it in airtight containers in the refrigerator for up to 5 days or the freezer for up to 3 months. Use as needed!

ZUCCHINI

Zucchini is third on my list of favorite vegetables. If you're keeping track, that's green beans, broccoli, and then zucchini. They cook so quickly, they have a great texture, and they're so versatile. I can put them in pasta, risotto, soups, and breads, and they make a great side salad with summer squash. However, they go bad pretty quickly and should be in the "eat sooner" category.

73. Chocolate Zucchini Bread

This recipe is great for using zucchini that's not quite appealing enough to cook dinner with, but is still perfect for baking. As with my (Overripe) Banana Bread (page 96), you're free to add extra chocolate chips or chopped walnuts. My favorite way to enjoy this, same as the banana bread, is to toast a thick slice of it in a skillet and top with lots of peanut butter.

MAKES 1 LOAF

Cooking oil spray (optional)
¼ cup olive oil
⅓ cup almond milk
1 cup brown sugar
2 teaspoons pure
    vanilla extract
1 tablespoon ground flaxseeds
1 cup grated zucchini (about
    1 medium zucchini)
1½ cups all-purpose flour

¼ cup unsweetened
    cocoa powder
½ teaspoon baking powder
½ teaspoon baking soda
½ teaspoon salt
1 teaspoon ground cinnamon
¼ cup vegan chocolate
    chips (optional)
¼ cup chopped
    walnuts (optional)

1. Preheat the oven to 375°F. Line a standard 9-by-4-inch loaf pan with compostable parchment paper or spray it with oil.
2. Whisk together the olive oil, almond milk, brown sugar, vanilla, and flaxseeds in a large bowl until well combined.
3. Gently blot the grated zucchini with a towel to remove excess moisture, then add to the bowl. Stir everything together.

4. In a small bowl, whisk together the flour, cocoa powder, baking powder, baking soda, salt, and cinnamon.

5. Pour the flour mixture into the zucchini mixture and stir gently until just combined, being careful not to overmix the batter. If desired, fold in the chocolate chips and/or walnuts. Then, pour the batter into the prepared loaf pan.

6. Bake for 45 to 55 minutes, until a toothpick inserted into the center comes out clean. Remove from the oven and allow the loaf to cool in the pan for a few minutes, then transfer it to a cooling rack and let cool before eating.

CHAPTER 5

PROLONGING YOUR PANTRY

We've covered what to do with leftover cranberries, citrus peels, porch pumpkins, and herbs, but what about our pantry? Some commonly tossed pantry items like stale chips and crackers could be given a second chance.

In this chapter, we'll bring stale bread back to life, make soft chips and crackers crunchy again, and use every last drop of those nearly empty jars. Turning the last bits of your peanut butter jar into overnight oats or a peanut sauce, shaking the mustard jar to make a salad dressing or marinade, and using leftover pickle juice for quick pickles or even creating a jam-jar cocktail.

These recipes truly embody the zero-waste philosophy aiming to make the absolute most out of what you have in the most delicious way possible!

BREAD

Globally, bread is recognized as one of the most wasted food items. Let's take a look at wasted bread around the world. In the United Kingdom, the campaign organization Love Food Hate Waste identifies bread as the most wasted food item in households, amounting to around 24 million slices discarded daily. Similarly, a study from the University of Borås in Sweden found that 80,000 tons of bread was wasted each year. The EPA in the United States reports that bread is one of the most wasted food items, and in Ireland, 41 percent of people admit to throwing out bread.

Let's aim to change this!

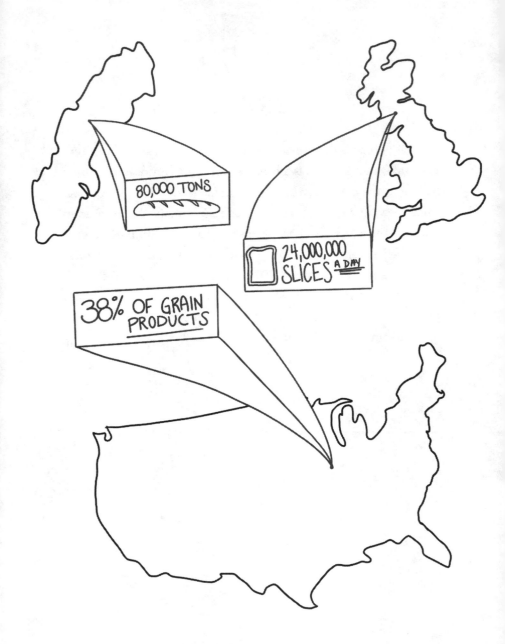

74. Freeze Your Bread

One of the best ways to keep your bread products fresh is by storing them in the freezer. When you get home from the grocery store or market, slice your bread if it hasn't already been sliced. Then, store it in the freezer. Defrost pieces as needed. Bread slices defrost quickly, and most toasters have a setting to defrost the bread. It's the easiest way to prevent your bread from molding or going stale.

75. Revive Stale Bread

If your bread has already gone stale, you can try to remedy it. Running your bread under cold water is an easy trick to restore some moisture and make your bread temporarily softer.

1. Lightly wet the stale bread under cold running water. Avoid soaking it or making it too wet, as this can make the bread soggy.
2. Once the bread is damp, place it directly on the rack in a 350°F oven at a low temperature for a few minutes. This helps evaporate the surface moisture and slightly crisp up the bread.
3. Keep a close eye on the bread while it's in the oven, to prevent it from burning. The exact time needed will vary depending on the size and thickness of the bread, but it should take only a few minutes.
4. Once the bread has been in the oven for a short time, remove it and let it cool slightly before consuming.

76. Croutons

When bread goes stale, it starts to lose its moisture, which results in its being hard and chewy. Croutons and bread crumbs are an excellent solution for this because, for them, you need dry and crisp bread without any moisture. Both are easy to whip up, delicious, and look pretty impressive. If you store them in an airtight container, they should maintain well in your pantry for up to 1 week. Personally, I like herbed bread crumbs on my salad so I get a little crunch with every bite, and big croutons on top of my soup.

YIELD VARIES

Stale bread

Olive oil

Dried rosemary

Salt and freshly ground

black pepper

1. Preheat the oven to 350°F. Cut the stale bread into your desired size chunks.
2. Place the bread chunks in a bowl and toss with enough olive oil to ensure all the pieces are coated evenly. Sprinkle with your desired amount of rosemary, salt, and pepper, adjusting the amounts according to personal preference.
3. Spread the seasoned chunks in a single layer on a dry baking sheet. Bake for 15 to 25 minutes, depending on the size of the chunks. Longer bake times will be required for larger chunks to achieve your desired crispiness.

4. Check the croutons periodically and remove from the oven when they have reached your desired level of crispness. Allow the croutons to cool before serving.

> **Pro Tip:** *To make delicious bread crumbs, instead of cutting into chunks, blitz your bread in a blender or food processor until it reaches your desired crumb consistency. Drizzle with a bit of olive oil, add your desired seasonings, and bake until nice and crispy.*

77. French Toast

Stale bread also works well for French toast because the moisture loss makes the bread more absorbent. This allows the bread to soak up the custard mixture more easily and it won't become overly soggy and fall apart.

SERVES 2

1 cup plant-based milk, such as almond milk or soy milk

2 tablespoons almond or oat flour

1 tablespoon pure maple syrup

1 teaspoon pure vanilla extract

½ teaspoon ground cinnamon

¼ teaspoon ground nutmeg

Pinch of salt

Vegan butter for frying

4 slices stale bread

1. Whisk together the milk, almond flour, maple syrup, vanilla, cinnamon, nutmeg, and salt in a medium bowl until well combined.
2. Heat a 12-inch skillet or griddle over medium heat and add a small amount of the butter to melt and coat the surface.
3. Dip a slice of stale bread into the milk mixture, ensuring it is evenly coated on both sides. Place the soaked bread slice in the pan and cook for 2 to 3 minutes per side, until golden brown and crispy. Repeat until all the bread is fried, one at a time.
4. Remove the French toast from the pan and transfer to serving plates. Serve warm with your favorite toppings, such as fresh fruit and pure maple syrup.

CAKE

The following is my husband's favorite scraptastic recipe. I bought his birthday cake a few days before his birthday, just so it could sit out and get a little stale. I've also made this recipe when a batch of cupcakes for a party didn't turn out right. So, this recipe will save the day whether you have a cake that's getting stale—meaning it's no more than 4 days old—or if your cake is stuck to the bottom of the pan.

NOTE: *This recipe is not designed for cakes with fresh fruit. Fresh fruit can go bad more quickly than in 4 days.*

78. Cake Truffles

A cake truffle is basically the same thing as a cake pop, but without the pop. I bring them to parties a lot because it's easier to enjoy a bite-size treat and you don't have to worry about forks, plates, or dishes! When it comes to making the chocolate coating for this recipe, I prefer a really dark or semisweet chocolate because there's already a lot of sugar in the icing.

This recipe is very flexible, based on what you have! I've made these truffles with two slices of cake, 24 broken cupcakes, and even a 7-inch intentionally-left-on-the-counter-to-get-stale cake. Just remember that you need to balance the icing level with the moisture of your cake. Add more icing if your cake is really stale, and less if you're just covering up a baking accident fresh out of the pan. If your cake has A LOT of icing on it, out of an abundance of caution, remove some and set it to the side. You can always add more icing later.

For this recipe, we'll use a 7-inch-wide two-layer cake, which pairs nicely with a 10-ounce bag of chocolate chips.

MAKES APPROXIMATELY 18 TRUFFLES

One stale 7-inch-wide, iced
  2-layer cake
One 10-ounce bag vegan
  chocolate chips

1. Crumble the stale cake, with its icing, into a large bowl, ensuring there are no large chunks. Use your hands or a fork to break it down into fine crumbs.

2. Take a small portion of the cake crumbs and roll them between your palms to form a compact ball. Repeat this process until all the cake crumbs have been rolled into equal-size balls.

3. Place the cake balls in the fridge for a few hours, or the freezer for 30 minutes, to let them harden. It will make them easier to dip into the chocolate

4. Melt the chocolate in a microwave-safe bowl or using a double boiler. If using a microwave, heat the chocolate in short intervals, stirring in between, until fully melted and smooth.

5. One at a time, dip the cake balls into the melted chocolate, using a fork or two spoons to fully coat them. Allow any excess chocolate to drip off.

6. Place the coated cake truffles in a single layer on a compostable parchment–lined plate or baking sheet.

7. Chill in the refrigerator for at least an hour, to allow the chocolate to harden.

8. Once hardened, transfer the cake truffles into an airtight container and store them for up to 5 days in the refrigerator until ready to serve!

CHIPS, COOKIES, CRACKERS

If you have boxes of chips, cookies, or crackers in your pantry, they might go stale. Your first thought might be to toss them, but as long as they aren't growing mold or totally falling apart, and as along as they don't smell bad, they can easily be revived. These crisp goodies often go stale because they absorb moisture from the surrounding environment, which can cause them to become soft and lose their desired texture.

The thing is, half-opened plastic bags inside of boxes aren't the best at preserving freshness. Keeping these items in an airtight container will help minimize their exposure to air and moisture, thus prolonging their freshness. But if your food does go stale, here are a few ways you can revive it before composting.

79. Revive Stale Snacks

This trick will work for all types of chips, crackers, and crunchy cookies, such as gingersnaps. It's also a great way to utilize the preheating energy your oven provides.

Stale tortilla chips, crackers, or crunchy cookies

1. Spread the stale snack evenly on a baking sheet and place the baking sheet in a cold oven.
2. Then, preheat your oven to 400°F. Allow the oven to reach temperature and then reheat the snack for about 5 minutes after your oven hits 400°F, or until crisp and heated through.
3. Remove from the oven and let the snack cool slightly on its pan before serving. Enjoy your revived snack that is now as good as new!

80. Stale Cookies Crust

Once when I was in a musical, a bag of gingersnaps was left on the snack table backstage for far too long. The once-crispy cookies were quite bendy, so it was evident they had gone pretty stale. But the good news: I took them home and made an incredible lemon-ginger vegan cheesecake with them. It was such a hit with friends that I was asked to make it for two more events after that, and I think the stale cookie crust was really the secret ingredient. This crust can be used for both chilled and baked cheesecakes or tarts.

MAKES ONE 8-INCH CRUST

8 tablespoons unsalted vegan butter, melted, plus more for pan

14 ounces cookies

1 tablespoon pure maple syrup

Pinch of salt

1. Preheat your oven to 350°F. Butter a springform cake pan with vegan butter or, alternatively, butter and line a regular 8-by-8-inch square cake pan with compostable parchment paper.
2. Place the cookies in a blender or food processor and blend until they form fine crumbs.
3. Combine the cookie crumbs, maple syrup, melted butter, and a pinch of salt in a medium bowl. Mix well until evenly moistened.
4. Press the mixture evenly into the bottom of the prepared pan.
5. Bake for approximately 15 minutes, or until golden brown.

6. Remove from the oven and let cool to room temperature. Once the crust is baked and cooled, it is ready to be used as a base for your desired filling.

7. If making a chilled pie, you can proceed with adding the filling and refrigerating it. If you prefer a baked pie, you can add the filling and return it to the oven for further baking per your pie recipe's instructions.

81. Chip and Cracker Breaded Tofu

Whether your chips are stale, you have too many crumbs at the bottom of a bag, or both, you should try this recipe to create a delicious crispy dredge for tofu. It's one of my absolute favorite ways to eat tofu. You can try this recipe with just one type of chip or cracker, such as potato chips, tortilla chips, or saltines. But if you have a lot of crumbs in a few different bags, you can also try a mixture. Just go for an even crumb size.

SERVES 4

Cooking oil for frying
1 cup of assorted chips and
   crackers of your choice
1 cup of all-purpose flour
Seasonings of your choice
   (e.g., salt, freshly ground
   black pepper, paprika,
   garlic powder)

1 cup of nondairy milk (e.g.,
   almond milk, soy milk)
1 block of firm tofu, sliced
   into desired shapes (*I just
   do rectangles, but if you
   can make dino nuggets, I
   mean why not?*)

1. Heat the oil in a skillet over medium heat.
2. Crush your chips into fine crumbs, then transfer the crumbs to a shallow bowl or plate.
3. In a separate shallow bowl, combine the flour and your chosen seasonings. Into another shallow bowl, pour your milk. Prepare a dredging station by lining up your bowls so the flour mixture is first, followed by the milk and then the chip crumbs.

4. Dip each slice of tofu into the flour mixture, coating it evenly. Shake off any excess flour. Next, dip the tofu into the milk, ensuring it is fully coated. Transfer the tofu to the bowl with the crushed chips and crackers. Press the crumbs onto the tofu, ensuring they adhere well and form a crispy coating.

5. Working in batches, carefully place the breaded tofu slices into the hot oil, being cautious to not overcrowd the pan. Fry the tofu on each side until golden brown and crispy. This usually takes 3 to 4 minutes per side.

6. Once cooked, remove the tofu from the oil and place it on a cooling rack that has been set atop a baking pan, to let any excess oil drain off. Repeat the process with the remaining tofu slices.

Serve the fried tofu immediately while still hot and crispy. It pairs well with dipping sauces or can be used in various dishes.

NOTE: *This recipe also works well with homemade bread crumbs (see the Pro Tip on page 186).*

82. Reheat Fries

I know a lot of people who won't take fries home from restaurants because they don't reheat well. And they absolutely don't, if you're using a microwave. Instead try this for bringing your leftovers back to life.

1. Preheat your oven to 400°F. Arrange the leftover fries in a single layer on a baking sheet. It's important to not overcrowd them, to ensure even heating.

2. Bake the fries for 5 to 10 minutes, or until hot and crispy. The exact time will depend on the thickness of the fries and the desired level of crispness. Check on them frequently to avoid overcooking or burning them. You may need to flip them halfway through the reheating process for even browning.

3. Once the fries are hot and crispy, remove from the oven and let cool slightly before serving.

JARS

I don't know about you, but I haven't met a jar I don't like. I like to think of myself as a collector. When I was a kid I used to collect rocks. I think that's called a crystal collection now, or maybe I just had way too much rose quartz. I collect playbills from all of the musicals and plays I see. And I collect glass jars.

I specifically like to buy food items like jam, pickles, peanut butter, and pasta sauce in glass jars so I can upcycle these versatile vessels. Could they be recycled? Maybe. It depends on how well glass is recycled in your area. But why recycle them when they're so useful?

Recently, I added pumps to two kombucha bottles and they're the most beautiful duo, dishing out hand soap and lotion in my bathroom. You can attach spray nozzles to them for homemade cleaning products, use them to store leftovers, drinking glasses, any type of organization from the bathroom to the basement, perfect vehicles for homemade gifts, and good to give out to guests to send home with leftovers and so much more.

But before we get to the upcycling phase, the jars need to be clean, and before we get to the cleaning phase, we enter what I like to call . . . *the last-drop phase*. This is where there's still some good stuff hanging around the sides of the jar. Each of these recipes is designed so you can get every last drop of goodness out of your jar.

83. Spicy Jam Jar Glaze

Surprisingly, leftover jam can be quite versatile. When you get down to the bottom of a strawberry jam jar, you can pour in some homemade almond milk for a creamy strawberry milk. Or try adding in a scoop of vegan vanilla ice cream or your morning yogurt. Another great way to utilize the last bits of your jam: make this delicious sweet, smoky, and savory glaze that's perfect for marinating tofu for a stir-fry or brushing on top of a cauliflower before you roast it.

SERVES 1

1 tablespoon vinegar, such as Homemade Apple Scrap Vinegar (page 84)
1 tablespoon harissa paste
1 tablespoon soy sauce

1 teaspoon grated garlic
1 teaspoon grated fresh ginger

EQUIPMENT
Almost empty jam jar

1. Combine the apple cider vinegar, harissa paste, soy sauce, garlic, and ginger in an almost empty jam jar. Secure the lid tightly on the jar.
2. Shake the jar vigorously until all the ingredients are well combined and form a smooth glaze. Taste and adjust the seasonings according to your preference. You can add more harissa paste for spiciness or adjust the other ingredients to balance the flavors.
3. Once the glaze is ready, use it to coat or glaze your preferred dish. It works particularly well on cauliflower, adding a tangy and spicy kick.

84. Jam Cocktail Mixer

This is certainly the most festive way to use up the last few bits of a jam jar.

MAKES 1 OR 2 MOCKTAILS OR COCKTAILS

Plain seltzer water

EQUIPMENT
Almost empty jam jar

1. Pour the seltzer water into your almost empty jam jar, leaving some space at the top for mixing.
2. Stir the mixture well to incorporate the jam into the sparkling water and ensure that the jam is evenly distributed throughout. Top up with more seltzer and enjoy, or serve the fruit-infused sparkling water in separate glasses, adding vodka or tequila.

85. Jam Vinaigrette

This recipe is so versatile and perfect to pair with different types of salad. Pair a strawberry jam vinaigrette with a fresh strawberry summer salad or pair a pear dressing with a fall salad with roasted sweet potatoes and walnuts. Feel free to experiment with different vinegars or add herbs and spices to customize the flavor of the dressing. Maybe try the Strawberry Top Vinegar (page 104) with your strawberry jam. Remember to keep the dressing refrigerated and use it within a reasonable time frame.

MAKES 2 SERVINGS

1 teaspoon Dijon mustard

1 tablespoon balsamic or red wine vinegar, such as Leftover Red Wine Vinegar (page 227)

2 tablespoons extra-virgin olive oil

Kosher salt and freshly ground black pepper

EQUIPMENT
Almost empty jam jar containing about 1 tablespoon jam

1. Add the Dijon mustard, vinegar, and olive oil to your almost empty jam jar.
2. Secure the lid tightly on the jar and shake the jar vigorously until all the ingredients are well combined and the dressing has emulsified. Taste the dressing and add salt and pepper to taste.
3. Store the jar of homemade salad dressing in the refrigerator and use within 5 days.

86. Peanut Butter Jar Overnight Oats

My favorite part about getting a new peanut butter jar is knowing what I have to look forward to when it runs out. Either I'll give it to my dog to lick clean, which is adorable and incredibly water efficient because jars should be pretty clean before recycling them, or I'll make these overnight oats. This is a perfect make-ahead breakfast for busy mornings, and you can heat them up if you don't like cold oats. If you want to bulk these up even more, add a little extra plant-based milk and some vegan protein powder.

SERVES 2

1 cup oats

2 tablespoons flaxseeds

2 teaspoons chia seeds

1 cup plant-based milk, such as almond milk or soy milk

EQUIPMENT

Almost empty peanut butter jar

1. Add the oats, flaxseeds, and chia seeds to a clean, almost empty peanut butter jar. Then, add the milk. The amount of milk can be adjusted based on personal preference for the consistency of the oats.
2. Stir the ingredients in the jar until well combined, then seal the jar with a lid and place in the refrigerator.
3. Allow the jar of overnight oats to sit in the fridge overnight, or for at least 6 to 8 hours, so the oats can absorb the liquid.
4. In the morning, take the jar from the refrigerator and give it a good stir before enjoying!

87. Leftover Peanut Butter Peanut Sauce

If you're not a big fan of overnight oats, you can try making this peanut sauce instead. You can use this as a dipping sauce, for stir-fries, or for a noodle salad.

SERVES 2

2 tablespoons soy sauce

1 tablespoon rice vinegar

1 tablespoon pure maple syrup

1 garlic clove, minced

1 teaspoon grated fresh ginger

¼ teaspoon red pepper flakes (optional)

Warm water, as needed, to adjust consistency

EQUIPMENT

Almost empty jam jar containing about 2 tablespoons peanut butter

1. Add the soy sauce, rice vinegar, maple syrup, minced garlic, grated ginger, and red pepper flakes (if desired) to the peanut butter jar.

2. Place the lid on the jar and shake it to combine all the ingredients. If the sauce is too thick, you can add warm water, a tablespoon at a time, until you reach your desired consistency.

3. Taste the sauce and adjust the seasoning according to your preference. You can add more soy sauce for saltiness, maple syrup for sweetness, or red pepper flakes for spiciness.

4. Store any leftover sauce in a sealed container in the refrigerator for up to 1 week.

88. Mustard Jar Vinaigrette

This is one of my favorite dressings of all time. I wouldn't recommend using yellow mustard, but it works great with Dijon, stoneground, deli, and spicy. Hot deli mustard is currently my favorite, and I actually used all of my mustard, making this dressing over and over. When I was almost out of mustard, I then got to use the last bits to make this recipe one last time in the jar.

My favorite way to use this dressing is on a pita pizza. You use a pita as the base and put it in the oven till it gets nice and crispy. Then, you top with hummus, and a Greek salad tossed in this dressing. It might sound odd, but it's delicious!

SERVES 2

Juice of ½ lemon
1 tablespoon olive oil
1 teaspoon pure maple syrup
Salt and freshly ground
    black pepper

EQUIPMENT
Almost empty mustard jar
    containing about
    2 tablespoons mustard

1. Squeeze the lemon juice into your mustard jar. Add the olive oil and maple syrup, then season with salt and pepper to taste.
2. Close the lid and give the jar a good shake to combine all the ingredients. Use on your favorite salad, pita pizza, and more.

89. Pickle Jar Quick Pickled Onions

If you have leftover pickle juice after you finish a jar of pickles, you can make a quick second pickle with any vegetable you want. I love pickled carrots, onions, and green beans. These quick pickles may not have the same intensity of flavor as traditional pickles, and they're meant to be stored in the refrigerator and consumed within 2 weeks, but they're absolutely delicious!

SERVES 4

Vegetables of your choice, such as cucumbers, carrots, onions, or cauliflower

Leftover pickle juice

Optional: additional spices or herbs for flavor, such as garlic, dill, peppercorns

EQUIPMENT

Almost empty pickle jar containing its leftover pickle juice

1. Wash the vegetables thoroughly and slice them into your desired shapes or sizes. For cucumbers, you can slice them into rounds or spears. For carrots, you can cut them into sticks or coins. Onions can be sliced thinly, and cauliflower can be separated into florets.

2. Place the sliced vegetables into your pickle jar containing the leftover pickle juice and make sure they are all fully submerged. If the pickle juice is not enough to cover the vegetables, you can add a small amount of water or vine-

gar to top it off. If desired, you can add additional spices or herbs to enhance the flavor. Popular choices include garlic cloves, dill sprigs, or peppercorns. Experiment with different combinations to find your favorite flavors.

3. Seal the jar with a tight-fitting lid and give it a gentle shake to distribute the ingredients.

4. Place the jar in the refrigerator and let the vegetables marinate in the pickle juice for at least a few hours or overnight. The longer they sit, the more pronounced the flavor will be.

90. Repurpose Your Used Jars

After we've passed the last-drop phase, it's time to move on to the upcycling phase. When upcycling the jars, aesthetically speaking, I prefer to remove the labels. If you have a jar with a plastic label, it should peel away easily with your bare hands and in one piece. For the leftover residue, use a little bit of dish soap with some steel wool. Dampen the bottle, scrub away, and rinse. All of the residue should come away quickly and easily.

If you have a paper label—typically a label that's very difficult to remove with your bare hands—try this instead.

Container, such as a Stasher® silicone bag or a large bowl	Dish soap, such as Castille soap
Water	Jar with stubborn label/sticky residue

1. Prepare a container, such as a Stasher® bag or a large bowl, by filling it with warm water and a few pumps of dish soap. Ensure the container is large enough to fully submerge the jar.

2. Place the jar with the stubborn label or sticky residue inside the container, ensuring it is fully immersed in the soapy water. Allow the jar to soak overnight. This extended soaking time will help loosen the adhesive and make the label easier to remove.

3. The next day, remove the jar from the soapy water. You will notice that the label is now much easier to peel off, and any

sticky residue should be significantly reduced. Gently peel off the label from the jar.

4. Once the label is removed, thoroughly rinse the jar under running water to remove any remaining soap residue. If you still have leftover residue, use the steel wool method described above.

5. Dry the jar, using a clean towel, or allow it to air dry completely before using it for storage or any other purpose.

NOTE: *If your tomato sauce jar smells too much like spaghetti sauce, wash it in hot soapy water, then let it dry open in direct sunlight. Place the lid out there as well, face up. The sun should help kill any residual odors.*

CHICKPEA AQUAFABA

Beans are extremely versatile, so versatile in fact that you can even use the liquid they're cooked in to create more amazing recipes. Let's talk about bean water. You can use other types of bean water to make aquafaba, but chickpea water is the most common.

Aquafaba is the liquid that comes from cooked beans or chickpeas. Its usefulness was discovered by a French chef named Joël Roessel in 2014. He found that the starchy liquid could be used as an alternative to egg whites in various culinary applications.

It's important to note that the consistency and strength of aquafaba can vary depending on the type of beans used and the cooking method. You can use the liquid from homemade beans, but the liquid from canned chickpeas is the most common because it tends to have a more consistent texture. You can store the liquid in the fridge for 3 to 4 days if you aren't using it immediately.

91. Egg-Free Royal Icing

I had a decorate-your-own cookie bar at my Christmas party last year, with reusable piping bags filled with different icing colors. It was a huge hit. This icing will completely harden when dry, like a traditional royal icing, and freezes very well.

MAKES ABOUT 5 CUPS

½ cup aquafaba (liquid from canned chickpeas)

1 tablespoon fresh lemon juice or cream of tartar

1 tablespoon pure vanilla extract

4 cups powdered sugar

Food coloring (optional)

1. Combine the aquafaba, lemon juice, and vanilla in a large bowl. Mix together using a whisk or electric mixer on high until soft peaks have formed, 5 to 10 minutes.
2. Gradually add the powdered sugar, about 1 cup at a time, incorporating it on low speed. If desired, add food coloring, and mix well until the color is evenly distributed.
3. Decorate your cookies or other treats, and allow the icing to dry and set completely before serving or storing.
4. Store any unused royal icing in an airtight container in the fridge or freeze.

NOTE: *When making this, you might want to use a little bit more or less powdered sugar to get your preferred consistency.*

92. Aquafaba Chocolate Mousse

This is an easy dessert you can whip up when you want a little treat, or it's impressive to serve to guests in mini ramekins. This will keep in the fridge for two to three days. Before serving, you can garnish the mousse with whipped cream, shaved chocolate, or fresh berries, if desired.

MAKES 4 SMALL RAMEKINS

1 cup semisweet or dark vegan chocolate chips

1 cup aquafaba (liquid from canned chickpeas)

½ teaspoon fresh lemon juice or cream of tartar

¼ cup sugar

1 teaspoon pure vanilla extract

Pinch of salt

Optional toppings: whipped cream, shaved vegan chocolate, fresh berries

1. Melt the chocolate chips using a double boiler or by microwaving in a microwave-safe bowl in short intervals, stirring until smooth. Set aside to cool slightly, but keep an eye out to make sure the chocolate doesn't harden. Your chocolate should still be pourable when you fold it in.
2. Combine the aquafaba, lemon juice, sugar, vanilla, and salt in a large bowl. Using an electric mixer or stand mixer, beat the aquafaba mixture on high speed until it forms stiff peaks. This may take 5 to 7 minutes.
3. Gently fold the melted chocolate into the whipped aquafaba until well combined. Be careful not to overmix, which could deflate the mixture.

4. Divide the mousse among individual serving dishes or ramekins. Cover and refrigerate for at least 2 hours, or until set and chilled.

NOTE: *If for some reason your mousse deflates (it happens even to the best of us), pop this into the freezer to turn it into ice cream. If you have reusable ice pop molds, this will make a great Fudgsicle-style treat!*

93. More Ways to Use Aquafaba

Egg White Replacement: Aquafaba can be whipped to create a foam that mimics the texture and properties of whipped egg whites. It can be used in such recipes as meringues, macarons, mousses, and marshmallows.

Binder in Baked Goods: Aquafaba can act as a binding agent in such recipes as cakes, cookies, and brownies. It helps hold the ingredients together and provides moisture.

Vegan Mayonnaise: Aquafaba can be emulsified with oil and other ingredients to create a creamy and egg-free mayonnaise.

Ice Cream: Aquafaba can be incorporated into vegan ice cream recipes to improve texture and mimic the creaminess of traditional ice cream.

94. Use Bean Liquid!

If you're making soup or stew, don't drain your beans. The bean water will add a rich and savory flavor, enhancing its overall taste and texture. The starches and proteins released during the cooking process will contribute to a thicker and more velvety texture. The bean water is also packed with nutrients, including soluble fiber, vitamins, and minerals.

MILK

Contrary to common belief, sour milk isn't bad or even spoiled. It just might not taste supergreat to drink, but it can still be used in cooking and baking. When dairy milk sours, it undergoes a natural process called fermentation, whereby the lactose in milk is converted into lactic acid by beneficial bacteria. This process gives sour milk its tangy taste and changes its texture.

Sour milk is an excellent substitute for buttermilk in recipes, adding a tangy flavor and helping to tenderize baked goods. It can also be used in pancake and waffle batters to enhance their texture and rise.

Sour milk can also be used to make such homemade dairy products as yogurt or cheese. The acid in sour milk helps curdle the milk proteins, creating a thick and creamy texture suitable for various dairy-based recipes.

Note: *It's important to clarify that the term "sour milk" refers to dairy-based milk that has naturally soured through fermentation. Milk that has developed mold, is chunky, or has an unpleasant odor should be discarded, as it may indicate spoilage or the presence of harmful bacteria.*

95. Sour Milk Mega Fluffy Pancakes

I've made these pancakes with sour soy milk and almond milk, but you can use any other type of sour milk you have on hand, including dairy milk. The tangy flavor of the sour milk adds a unique twist to the pancakes, making them fluffy and delicious.

MAKES APPROXIMATELY 6 MEDIUM PANCAKES

2 cups all-purpose flour
1 tablespoon baking powder
2 tablespoons sugar
Pinch of salt

1 cup sour milk
½ cup water
2 tablespoons oil, plus
more for pan

1. Whisk together the all-purpose flour, baking powder, sugar, and salt in a large bowl until well combined. In a medium bowl, Stir together the sour milk, water, and oil until evenly mixed.
2. Pour the milk mixture into the flour mixture and gently stir until just combined. Be careful not to overmix; a few lumps are okay. The batter should be thick and slightly lumpy.
3. Heat a large nonstick skillet or griddle over medium heat. Lightly oil the surface. Pour about ¼ cup of batter onto the skillet for each pancake. Cook until bubbles start to form on the surface of the pancakes and the edges look set, usually 2 to 3 minutes. Then, flip the pancakes, using a spatula, and cook for an additional 1 to 2 minutes, or until golden brown on both sides.

4. Remove the pancakes from the skillet and repeat the process with the remaining batter, adding more oil to the skillet, if needed.

5. Serve the sour milk pancakes warm with your favorite toppings, such as pure maple syrup, fresh fruits, or whipped cream.

NOTE: *If you're making pancakes for a crowd, keep your pancakes warm in the oven. Preheat your oven to 200°F so they'll all be piping hot and delicious for everyone at the same time.*

OATS

While growing up, I ate a lot of oatmeal for breakfast. My favorite was always the maple and brown sugar. Now, I make my own oatmeal depending on what's in season. During the summer, I enjoy peaches and cream oatmeal with crushed pecans. My go-to fall oatmeal is apple cinnamon with crushed walnuts. And my wild card oatmeal has been carrot cake oatmeal—surprisingly good and a great way to use up some wilting carrots!

I prefer to make homemade almond milk for my oatmeal, but if you make homemade oat milk, here are a few ways you can utilize your oat pulp.

96. Homemade Oat Milk

This is my favorite recipe for oat milk!

MAKES APPROXIMATELY 6 CUPS

1 cup rolled oats
6 cups water

Optional sweeteners
or flavorings: 1 to
2 tablespoons pure maple
syrup, pure vanilla extract,
or a couple of pitted dates,
for sweetness

1. Combine the rolled oats and water in a blender. If you'd like sweetened oat milk, add your choice of sweetener or flavoring at this stage.
2. Blend on medium speed for 30 to 45 seconds, until the mixture is well combined and the oats are broken down.
3. Place a nut milk bag, fine-mesh strainer, or cheesecloth over a clean bowl or jug. Pour the oat mixture through it to separate the liquid from any oat residue. To prevent the oat milk from becoming slimy, let gravity do most of the work and try to avoid oversqueezing.
4. Transfer the freshly made oat milk to a clean glass jar or bottle. Seal it and store in the refrigerator for up to 1 week.

NOTE: *Oat milk may naturally settle in the fridge, so give it a good shake before each use.*

97. Ideas for Leftover Oat Pulp

Oatmeal: This one's not rocket science, but you can cook your leftover oat pulp with your oats to make oatmeal.

Oat Flour: Spread the oat pulp on a dry baking sheet and bake it at a low temperature until completely dry. Once dry, place in a dry blender and blend the pulp into a fine powder to create homemade oat flour.

Gooey Cookies: Replace ⅓ cup of all-purpose flour with oat pulp in your favorite cookie recipe. Try this with chocolate chip cookies because an ooey-gooey oatmeal chocolate chip cookie is my favorite.

Oat Pulp Crackers: Mix the oat pulp with herbs, spices, and a binder, such as flaxseed or chia seeds. Spread the mixture thinly on a dry baking sheet and bake in a 375°F oven for about 15 minutes, until crispy.

Oat Milk Bath: Oatmeal baths are great for dry and itchy skin. Try using your leftover oat pulp instead. You can keep the oats in their straining bag so they don't clog your drain, and the oat pulp will release its natural properties, providing a calming and nourishing experience for your skin.

98. Oat Pulp Brownie Bites

These brownie bites are one of my favorite snacks. They make a delicious and nutritious snack for a quick energy boost throughout the day. Just make sure you've squeezed all the moisture out of your oat pulp. If it's too wet, your bites might not come together.

MAKES 12 BROWNIE BITES

12 pitted fresh dates
1 cup oat pulp
¾ cup walnuts
1 tablespoon unsweetened
　cocoa powder

Pinch of salt
Sesame seeds for
　garnish (optional)

1. Combine the dates, oat pulp, walnuts, cocoa powder, and salt in a food processor. Process the mixture until it forms a solid ball and the ingredients are well combined.
2. Take small portions of the mixture and roll them into 12 equal-size brownie balls, using your hands to shape them evenly.
3. Sprinkle the brownie balls with sesame seeds (if using), gently pressing them onto the surface of the brownies.
4. Refrigerate the bites for about 30 minutes to firm up before serving. Or store them in an airtight container in the refrigerator for up to 1 week.

ALMONDS

I really like to make almond milk. When you make it yourself, it's very creamy and so easy. But after making it, you're often left with almond pulp. You may not know what to do with this right away, but it's so versatile. You can use it in a lot of the same ways that you'd use your oat pulp, such as for cookies, crackers, and flour. But here are a few of my favorite recipes.

99. Almond Milk

This is my go-to recipe for almond milk and a great way to enjoy eating dairy-free!

MAKES APPROXIMATELY 6 CUPS

1 cup raw almonds

6 cups water

1 to 2 tablespoons of pure maple syrup, pure vanilla extract, or a couple of pitted dates for sweetness (optional)

1. Place the almonds in a bowl and cover them with water. Allow them to soak for at least 4 hours or overnight. This softens the almonds for easier blending. After soaking, drain and rinse the almonds.

2. Combine the soaked almonds and water in a blender. If you'd like sweetened almond milk, add your choice of sweetener or flavoring at this stage.

3. Blend at a low speed and gradually increase it to high. Blend for about 2 minutes, or until the mixture becomes smooth and creamy. Separate the liquid from the almond pulp with a nut milk bag, fine-mesh strainer, or cheesecloth over a clean bowl or jug. Squeeze or press the bag or cloth to extract as much milk as possible.

4. Transfer your almond milk to a clean glass jar or bottle, and store it in the refrigerator for up to 1 week.

NOTE: *Almond milk may naturally separate in the fridge, so give it a good shake before each use.*

100. Almond Dip

This spread is perfect to put out for parties. A lot of nondairy cheeses use nuts as a substitute because they're really creamy when blended. This recipe is a bit rustic depending on how much almond pulp you have, but I had about ½ cup. As always feel free to experiment with different herbs and spices to customize the flavor to your liking.

SERVES 2

Almond pulp (quantity may vary)
Juice of 1 medium lemon
2 teaspoons nutritional yeast
1 teaspoon garlic powder
1 teaspoon paprika

Salt and freshly ground black pepper
1 to 2 tablespoons fresh herbs (e.g., chives, basil, parsley, dill, and/or tarragon)

1. Combine the almond pulp, lemon juice, nutritional yeast, garlic powder, paprika, and your desired amount of salt and pepper in a medium bowl.
2. Add your herbs of choice and mix well to incorporate all the flavors. Taste the dip and adjust the seasonings, if needed, to suit your preference. Mix well.
3. Serve the almond pulp dip with crackers or use it as a flavorful dip for your favorite snacks.

WINE

I love to entertain, and without fail, at least one bottle of wine has been left uncorked overnight. All of that oxygen causes it to oxidize making it unpleasant to drink. The wine can develop a flat or vinegar-like taste. Which makes it perfect for creating your very own red wine vinegar.

101. Leftover Red Wine Vinegar

This recipe is perfect for homemade salad dressings, marinades, or any recipe that calls for vinegar.

YIELD VARIES

Leftover red wine

Vinegar, such as Homemade Apple Scrap Vinegar (page 84), with the mother[*]

1. Pour the leftover red wine into a clean jar, leaving some headspace at the top. Add approximately the same amount of apple cider vinegar with the mother as the amount of red wine in the jar.
2. Cover the opening of the jar with a swatch of cloth and secure it with a rubber band to allow airflow while keeping out insects and dust.
3. Place the jar in a cool, dry location, such as a cabinet or pantry. Let the mixture sit undisturbed for about 2 weeks to allow fermentation to occur. After a week, taste the vinegar. If it has reached your desired acidity and flavor, it is ready to use. If not, you can continue to ferment it for a bit longer.
4. Any time you have a bottle of red wine you can't finish, keep adding it to your red wine vinegar and you'll never run out.

---

[*] A vinegar mother is a viscous, gelatinous substance composed of bacteria and yeast. Healthy homemade vinegars should grow them, but you can also buy vinegar with the mother.

ACKNOWLEDGMENTS

I have always enjoyed being creative in the kitchen. My creativity mostly stemmed from having a severe dairy allergy and experimenting with fun ways to create things like ricotta out of tofu or a dairy-free cheesecake using the very limited dairy-free options available in Arkansas when I was a kid. Now you can easily buy dairy-free items at almost every supermarket, but my childhood instilled in me a joy for creativity in cooking.

I have many fond memories of spending time in the kitchen with my parents, from family dinners, parties, and both successful and unsuccessful attempts at making dairy dupes. So I have to thank them first. Both of my parents love food and love to cook. My dad was more experimental and creative, letting ingredients guide his decisions and rarely operating from a recipe. (He went through a chocolatier phase, which I would welcome back at any time.) My mom was a more precise cook; she would study recipes and create her own with the goal of making the best pie crust or the perfect French toast. Every time my friends came over, they would beg my parents to write a cookbook. While they may have yet to write one, I know this book wouldn't have existed without them. I can see their knowledge and love throughout these pages. Thank you both for teaching me to love and appreciate food and thank you for our time in the kitchen.

I also have to thank my amazing husband, Justin Norton, to whom this book is dedicated, for spending a lot of time with me in the kitchen this past year. This man did a lot of dishes! Beyond that, I am so grateful for your unending support. You have so fully believed in me from the day we met. You have done nothing but encourage me to reach for the stars and pursue my dreams. I love you so much.

Of course, I have to thank everyone at Countryman Press for publishing this book! I can't believe we just wrapped our second book together, and I'm so grateful for everyone on the team working to make this a reality. Plus, a shout-out to my agent, Amy Levenson, who's been with me from the beginning.

Thank you to my management—Nick, Shannon, Hala, and Amy—for keeping my entire life organized. I'm really not sure what I'd do without y'all.

And a huge thank-you to my friends and taste testers. Especially those of you who ate a pound of cabbage and kale before a three-hour dance rehearsal. Your contributions are recognized. But, really, I'm so grateful to each and every one of you for testing recipes and giving feedback, for our vegan supper club, and for your general love and support. Moving to Maine was one of the best things that's ever happened because I got to meet all of you.

Lastly, I'd like to acknowledge the amazing low-waste/zero-waste community. You all are so wonderful. The world is a better place because of you. You give me so much hope.

INDEX